LAND OF CONTENTION

LAND OF CONTENTION

Biblical Narratives and the Struggle for the Holy Land

ROB DALRYMPLE
Foreword by David A. deSilva

CASCADE *Books* • Eugene, Oregon

LAND OF CONTENTION
Biblical Narratives and the Struggle for the Holy Land

Copyright © 2024 Rob Dalrymple. All rights reserved. Except for brief quotations in critical publications or reviews, no part of this book may be reproduced in any manner without prior written permission from the publisher. Write: Permissions, Wipf and Stock Publishers, 199 W. 8th Ave., Suite 3, Eugene, OR 97401.

Cascade Books
An Imprint of Wipf and Stock Publishers
199 W. 8th Ave., Suite 3
Eugene, OR 97401

www.wipfandstock.com

PAPERBACK ISBN: 979-8-3852-2402-9
HARDCOVER ISBN: 979-8-3852-2403-6
EBOOK ISBN: 979-8-3852-2404-3

Cataloguing-in-Publication data:

Names: Dalrymple, Rob, author. deSilva, David A., foreword.

Title: Land of contention : biblical narratives and the struggle for the Holy Land / Rob Dalrymple; foreword by David A. deSilva.

Description: Eugene, OR: Cascade Books, 2024 | Includes bibliographical references.

Identifiers: ISBN 979-8-3852-2402-9 (paperback) | ISBN 979-8-3852-2403-6 (hardcover) | ISBN 979-8-3852-2404-3 (ebook)

Subjects: LCSH: Bible—Geography. | Bible—Criticism, interpretation, etc. | Land tenure—Biblical teaching. | Land tenure—Middle East.

Classification: BR115.L23 D50 2024 (paperback) | BR115.L23 (ebook)

VERSION NUMBER 102824

I want to dedicate this short book to all our friends in Israel, the West Bank, and Gaza—Israelis and Palestinians alike: Muslims, Christians, and Jews. My wife and I hold dear the moments we have shared with you, both in our home and yours. We share in your grief, knowing the turmoil you've endured for so long, especially as you have raised your children under such challenging circumstances.

In the wake of the October 7 attack and the ongoing assault on Gaza, we extend our deepest sympathies. We are distressed for the pain you're experiencing and the losses you've endured.

We are so sorry we did not raise our voices loudly or persistently enough in solidarity with you.

CONTENTS

Foreword by David A. deSilva | ix
Prologue | xv
My Story | xvii

PART 1: FRAMING THE CONVERSATION
1   Introduction | 3
2   Contrasting Kingdoms | 8
3   Understanding the Biblical Narrative and Our Role in It | 17

PART 2: A BIBLICAL THEOLOGY OF THE TEMPLE, THE PEOPLE, AND THE LAND
4   The Biblical Narrative and the Temple | 25
5   The Biblical Narrative and the People of God | 36
6   The Biblical Narrative and the Land | 55
7   Is This Replacement Theology? | 68
8   Conclusion | 70

PART 3: APPLICATION AND JUSTICE
9   Looking at the Israeli-Palestinian conflict through the lens of the kingdom of God | 77
10 Is It Okay to Critique Israel? Israel and Antisemitism | 79
11 The Miracle of 1948? | 85
12 Did God restore Israel to the land in 1948? | 88
13 Conclusion | 92

Resources | 95

FOREWORD

David A. deSilva

No, Rob Dalrymple is not antisemitic. He loves the people of Israel (just as he loves Jews in every country in which they find themselves). He just happens to love them in the way that Amos loved Israel rather than the way Amaziah loved Israel. Amaziah was the priest who oversaw the kingdom of Israel's sanctuary at Bethel under King Jeroboam I. As far as Amaziah was concerned, Israel, its leadership, and its institutions were sacred and above reproach: "Never again prophesy at Bethel, for it is the king's sanctuary, and it is a temple of the kingdom" (Amos 7:13). Begone, Amos. Criticism is off limits here. We're fine. It's fine. Everything's fine.

As far as Amos was concerned, Israel's practice, especially that of its leadership and empowered classes, had strayed dangerously far from doing justly, loving mercy, and walking humbly in God's presence (to borrow from another prophet). Nothing was more loving than for Amos to heed God's summons to him to warn Israel that it was no longer in alignment with God's plumb line (Amos 7:7–9).

> They trample the head of the poor into the dust of the earth, and push the afflicted out of the way (Amos 2:7).

Foreword

> Hate evil and love good, and establish justice in the gate;
> it may be that the LORD, the God of hosts, will be gracious to the remnant of Joseph (Amos 5:15).

Failure to heed some very valid criticisms led to a consequence that neither Amaziah nor Amos would ever have wanted for Israel: the northern kingdom of Israel was indeed sent "into exile away from its land" (Amos 7:17).

Rob is, however, not addressing Israelis or a general Western audience. He is primarily addressing Christians, calling us to examine whether the ideologies we have embraced in regard to the state of Israel and, in consequence, in regard to the families of Arabs who had lived in the land for generations and generations, are faithful to our Scriptures and to the values that Jesus established as nonnegotiable among his followers. He calls us to test our ideologies by their fruits, particularly whether they are contributing to (and leading us to promote) the flourishing of both Israelis and Palestinians, or whether they are contributing to (and leading us to promote) the oppression—the ghettoization, dispossession, perhaps eventually the elimination—of the latter for the sake of the flourishing of the former.

Early in this book, Rob poses the poignant question: "How should we respond when we find ourselves so entrenched in a theological conviction that we become unable or unwilling to 'Weep with those who weep' (Rom 12:15)?" Has our ideology hidden the humanness of the people of the land? Has it made us callous to the griefs they have experienced since 1948 and insensitive to the ongoing injustices that have been inflicted upon them, in our desire to "stand with Israel"? At the very least, we who claim Christ and, therefore, have been adopted into the "household of God" along with Palestinian Christians owe it to our brothers and sisters there to listen to their testimony concerning their experience and that of their parents and grandparents—and to allow their testimony to inform our own response.[1] They are flesh and blood; ideologies

---

1. Such testimonies are readily available to us. Follow up reading Rob's book with Munther Isaac, *The Other Side of the Wall: A Palestinian Christian Narrative of Lament and Hope* (Downers Grove, IL: InterVarsity, 2020); Mitri

are immaterial belief systems. We are always called to prioritize the former over the latter. We will be with those sisters and brothers for eternity; many of our ideological convictions will fall away when we come to see face-to-face rather than in the distorted reflections of this life (1 Cor 13:11–12).

Rob also poses important challenges to the very popular and powerful ideology of "Christian Zionism." He points out important ways in which Christians who have embraced this ideology display a strange eagerness to divorce the promises of the Old Testament with what New Testament authors themselves reckon to be the fulfillment of those promises and calls this eagerness into question. It is noteworthy that Amos ends with promises of the restoration of David's kingdom (9:11–12)—and that James, the brother of Jesus, sitting in Jerusalem itself, understands this promise to be fulfilled in the enthronement of his brother and the gathering together of a people drawn from both Jews and gentiles and not a promise about something that might happen in 1948 (see Acts 15:12–21). Why would we choose not to follow James's lead in this regard? Why would we abandon the guidance provided by the New Testament concerning the interpretation of the promises found in the Old Testament? Have we become wiser than James, Paul, John, or the author of Hebrews?

No doubt this tendency at the heart of Christian Zionism emerged at the outset out of a desire to advocate for the Jewish people, particularly those facing prejudice and pogroms in Europe and Russia, in their own quest to recover a homeland where they would no longer be dependent upon the hospitality—or lack thereof—of gentile nations. This tendency also reflects a measure of guilt, appropriately acknowledged, over the fact that many who claimed to be Christian failed to love the Jews in their midst with the same passion and longing that we find reflected, for example, in Paul's heart for them (Romans 9–11), contributing to the lack of hospitality as best and open hostility at worst. But it was not

---

Raheb, *Decolonizing Palestine: The Land, The People, The Bible* (Maryknoll, NY: Orbis, 2023); and Yohanna Katanacho, *The Land of Christ: A Palestinian Cry* (Eugene, OR: Pickwick, 2013).

the New Testament authors' understanding of the promises of God and their consummation in Jesus and the body of Jews and gentiles gathered in his name that was at fault. Rather, it was the Christians who chose lovelessness, disdain, and hostility—who did not sufficiently internalize the ethos that those New Testament authors sought to promote—who were at fault.

And in the present time, the ideology called "Christian Zionism" is no longer serving merely to advocate for the Jewish people and, more particularly, for the preservation of a nation-state that would serve as a homeland for the Jewish people (this is, of course, merely theoretical since the majority of Jews find themselves very much at home in their countries of citizenship throughout the world). Rather, it is serving to shield a particular, secular nation-state from the summons of the international community—which, of all things, ought to have been spearheaded by the whole of the Christian community!—to cease annexing the territory of their neighbors, to desist from the collective punishment of the people walled up in Gaza, and, above all at this moment, to stop considering the murder of so many civilians alongside the members of Hamas and allied insurgent groups acceptable "collateral damage."

There is a popular meme depicting an Israeli soldier kneeling with rifle raised, with a baby carriage tucked in behind him. Opposite him kneels a Hamas insurgent with rifle raised, a baby carriage in front of him, shielding him. This cartoon certainly points to a moral failure on the part of Hamas. But what has been the next panel in this cartoon time and time again? A dead Hamas soldier with a dead baby in front of him, both riddled with bullet holes from the Israeli soldier's rifle. We all know that this is the next scene, given the numbers of dead women and children in Gaza, and this certainly points to a moral failure on the part of Israel. Amos, along with all the prophets, showed us that, in order to love Israel well, we must call its people back when they act unjustly, not join Amaziah in calling Israel "off limits" when it comes to the prophetic speech that calls for the repentance that would set Israel on a path to a genuinely secure future.

Foreword

Rob particularly indicts us for our endorsement of military action, violence, and war. He writes, with biting irony, "While much of the world calls for a cease-fire and a just solution to the war on Gaza, it is mainly Western Christians who continue to encourage war and the destruction of Gaza. . . . Are not Christians to be on the side that advocates for a just peace instead of the side of war and violence?" So many Christians appear to have forgotten that violence begets violence and to treat as irrelevant the difference between the kingdom of God and the modus operandi of worldly powers, especially concerning the expression of love for one's enemies rather than the quest to dominate or eliminate one's enemies through violence and military action.

Rob leaves us with this question: "Has the church wholly capitulated to the ways of the world?" It doesn't call for a "yes" or a "no" answer. It calls for honest and prayerful self-examination in concert with a return to the instructions of Jesus to all who call him "Lord, Lord." And, yes, it calls for repentance and for a renewal of a more authentic Christian witness and practice—in a good many areas of life, no doubt, but also specifically in regard to our response to the nation-state of Israel. Israel has always had greater need, and God greater use, for an Amos than for an Amaziah.

"The Lord GOD has spoken; who can but prophesy?" (Amos 3:8).

PROLOGUE

Then Jesus said to him, "Put your sword back into its place; for all those who take up the sword shall perish by the sword" (Matt 26:52).[1]

THIS BRIEF WORK AIMS to propose an approach for how the church might proceed concerning justice issues in general, with a specific focus on Israel's present war on Gaza and the larger Israeli-Palestinian conflict. To be clear, I do not intend to suggest that I have all the answers. Instead, I hope to offer a framework within which we might engage in meaningful dialogue. This book will proceed in three parts.

In the first part, I provide a biblical foundation for understanding the mission of God's people. I sincerely hope everyone agrees with what I have to say here. I recognize, however, that applying such principles to the conflict in Israel-Palestine and the war on Gaza dramatically complicates matters. Therefore, in the latter two sections, I will address related justice issues regarding the conflict in Israel-Palestine.

In the second part, I will address the questions related to God's promises to Abraham, paying particular attention to the promises of descendants and the land. I recognize that some evangelicals struggle with the present conflict in Israel-Palestine. However, their convictions regarding God's covenant promises

---

1. All citations, unless otherwise noted, are from the NASB.

of family and land to the Jewish people cause them to side with Israel. I will argue that we must understand the promises of family (descendants) and land in light of the temple and the mission of God's people. I want to reiterate, however, that my genuine hope is that even if readers disagree with my convictions outlined in part two, we may still find a shared agreement on the justice issues impacting discussions related to Israel.

Finally, in part three, I will briefly address some additional issues, including how understanding the kingdom of God affects our advocacy with regard to this conflict. And, is it fair to critique Israel, or is that always antisemitism? And, finally, what about Israel's miraculous rebirth?

NB: The early portions of this work include several footnotes that readers should note. I will define a couple of terms (e.g., "Christian Zionism" and "Zionism," as well as "Jew/Jewish," and which designation I prefer when it comes to the land: "Israel" or "Palestine") and explain why I am using one designation for the land over another.

Rob Dalrymple
May 2024

MY STORY

I GREW UP IN a conservative, evangelical—though we did not call it evangelical back then—church.[1] For us, the Bible was preeminent.[2] Of course, its meaning was "evident" when "interpreted correctly," which meant that it must be understood "literally." Naturally, I was a Christian Zionist.[3] We considered the establishment of the state of Israel in 1948 as proof that a literal interpretation of the Bible was justified and that God has fulfilled his promises in our generation. It was evident to us that Jesus was about to return.

---

1. This church was great for me in many ways. As a child of a broken home, I found community in this church. I also found Jesus there.

2. I still hold to a very high view of the Bible.

3. Christian Zionism (CZ) is distinct from Zionism. Christian Zionism begins with the conviction that the biblical promises of family (descendants) and land to Abraham continue to apply to the physical descendants of Abraham, that is, the Jewish people. As such, CZs believe that the Jewish people are God's chosen people and that everyone is to bless them in order to be blessed by God (according to their reading of Genesis 12:1–3). Christian Zionists often, but not always, believe that the restoration of the Jewish people to the land in the twentieth century was an act of God (see chapters 11 and 12) and a sign of the imminent return of Jesus.

At the same time, CZ has become a political movement. Robert O. Smith suggests that CZ is a "political action, informed by specifically Christian commitment, to promote or preserve Jewish control over the geographic area now comprising Israel and Palestine" (Smith, *More Desired than Our Owne Salvation*, 2).

Zionism, on the other hand, is the belief that the Jewish people deserve a homeland (a state) of their own. This belief often entails the conviction that this Jewish state should be in the historic land of "Judea and Samaria."

During this period, I had little to no understanding of Palestine or Palestinians. If anything, my understanding was limited to the historical rise of Islam in the seventh century. I suppose that I just assumed that all of the non-Jewish population of the land were either expelled or converted to Islam. Concerning the current state of affairs, I was vaguely aware that Palestinians were engaged in terrorist activities—such as the blowing up of buses. Consequently, when my wife expressed concerns over my traveling to the land,[4] I assured her I would take a few steps back from the curb whenever I saw an approaching bus—which I did.

Two things that would later prove significant happened on my first trip to the land (2003). First, I witnessed some modest

4. Referring to "the land" is difficult in a work like this because many conversations are often politicized. The problem is that the designations "Israel," "Palestine," and "Judea and Samaria" all have limitations. To call the land "Israel" might be viewed as favoring the Jewish claims to the land. Moreover, the use of "Israel" might lead to confusion between the modern nation-state and the geographical territory. Since the modern state of Israel does not encompass the entirety of the land, and since the use of "Israel" could be confusing, I will endeavor to avoid using "Israel" to refer to the land unless the context is abundantly clear as to what I mean.

To refer to the land as "Palestine," which in many ways may be the best designation, might be viewed by some as favoring the Palestinians. This is unfortunate. After all, in the early twentieth century, the designation "Palestine" referred to the geographical area and Palestinians were the inhabitants even if they were Arabs or Jews. Finally, the problems with the label "Judea and Samaria" are manifold. For one, it is a highly politicized designation used by Zionists to assert their claims that the land is historically theirs—"Judea and Samaria" being titles that allude to the biblical designations for the land. Furthermore, the designation "Judea and Samaria" does not encompass all of the "promised land." Consequently, it is not an appropriate designation for this present work.

In the middle section of this work, I will employ "land of promise" or "the promised land." In doing so, I am referring to the biblical promise to Abraham and his descendants that God will give them a particular piece of land. Of course, this land's borders are never defined, but that is beside the point with respect to our concerns. When referring to the present land, I often opt for the designation "Palestine" because that is an historic designation as far back as the second century. In doing so, I ask for understanding and grace. I do not intend to be political when using this designation. The simple fact is that no suitable designation exists to avoid the politicization that encumbers these conversations.

injustices against Palestinian women and children. I did not attribute much significance to it, mainly because I did not understand what I was witnessing. I sensed that something was not right. Second, I learned there were Christians in the land—which only makes sense since Christianity originated there nearly two thousand years ago. However, I gave little thought to both of these. After all, I was in the midst of my doctoral studies.

My doctoral work was in the field of hermeneutics (a fancy way of saying "biblical interpretation"). I focused my research on the book of Revelation and John's depiction of the people of God.[5] My goal was to discern how John portrayed the people of God in the book of Revelation to reveal the underlying message he sought to convey to his audience. I concluded that the assorted portraits of the people of God in the book of Revelation (e.g., the 144,000, the Great Multitude, and the Two Witnesses) represented a unified description of the one people of God. I concluded that John's depiction of the people of God centered on their (and "our" by extension) core mission as God's people; namely, they were to both make God known and to suffer as a result of their witness. What I found to be incredibly insightful is that in the book of Revelation, John portrays the people of God in a manner that reflects Jesus. That is, the people of God (we) are imitators of Jesus.

After completing my studies, I was fortunate enough to revisit the land of Israel-Palestine (2008). During this trip, I began to observe more significant injustices toward the Palestinians. I learned not only that Christians were in this land but also that Christians had a significant presence there. These two factors triggered an existential crisis for me, for I realized that the suffering of the Palestinians, including Palestinian Christians, was, in some measure, attributed to people like myself. You see, I knew that the unwavering conviction, which I adhered to as a young man, that the Jewish[6] people were God's chosen people and that the Bible

---

5. This work was later published as *Revelation and the Two Witnesses*.

6. This is another tricky word. Most everyone understands its meaning, but a little nuancing may be necessary. Technically, the descendants of Abraham extend well beyond the Jewish people—even though many conceive of the

promises a blessing upon all who bless them led many American Christians to significantly influence the US government and its support for the state of Israel. There are indeed many reasons why the US supports the state of Israel. One of them, however, is undeniably the evangelical support.

What I had come to understand during this trip to the land was a stark reality: the unwavering support of Israel by evangelical[7] Christians in the West was enabling Israel's oppression of the Palestinian people. Much more could be said here—much of which I have done throughout a series of livestreams, webinars, podcasts, and blog posts.[8] Israel claims that the occupation of the Palestinians (the West Bank and Gaza) is necessary for security reasons. What I was witnessing, however, suggested that Israel's security concerns were, in part, the result of their oppressive occupation. Thus, the perfect storm. Israel's security concerns result in an oppressive occupation. The oppressive occupation intensifies Israel's security concerns as the Palestinian resistance increases (the oppressed can only handle so much). The more the Palestinians resist, the more oppressive the occupation. And so on.[9] The weight

---

Jewish people as the only descendants of Abraham. After all, Ishmael and Esau are direct descendants of Abraham. However, they are not considered part of the chosen people nor the recipients of the covenant promises. But leaving that aside, we must also recognize that the designation "Jewish" refers to the members of the southern tribes. Meanwhile, "Israel" came to mean the members of the northern tribes. Today, "Jewish" and "Israel" are often conflated. In fact, I will use "Israel" and "Jewish" interchangeably at times—even though this may not be completely accurate. For further discussions of "Israel" and "Jew" and related terms, see Jason A. Staples, *The Idea of Israel in Second Temple Judaism: A New Theory of People, Exile, and Israelite Identity* (Cambridge: Cambridge University Press, 2021); and *Paul and the Resurrection of Israel: Jews, Former Gentiles, Israelites* (Cambridge: Cambridge University Press, 2024).

7. Christian support for Israel transcends evangelicalism. Since, I associate myself to some extent with evangelicalism, I will be focusing on evangelical support for Israel in this work.

8. The resources associated with my work at Determinetruth, including the blog posts, YouTube videos, and the podcast, can be found on determinetruth.com. See QR codes linked to Determinetruth in the appendix of this book.

9. For further discussion of the context of this conflict, see the five-part series of livestreams in the playlist "A Brief Introduction to Israel-Palestine" on

of this realization brought me to tears. It was then that I realized I needed to engage with this issue.

---

the Determinetruth YouTube channel.

PART 1

FRAMING THE CONVERSATION

1

INTRODUCTION

Genesis 12:1–3, "Now the Lord said to Abram, Go forth from your country, And from your relatives, And from your father's house, To the land which I will show you; And I will make you a great nation, And I will bless you, And make your name great; And so you shall be a blessing; And I will bless those who bless you, And the one who curses you I will curse. And in you all the families of the earth will be blessed."

Genesis 15:18, "On that day the Lord made a covenant with Abram, saying, 'To your descendants I have given this land, From the river of Egypt as far as the great river, the river Euphrates.'"

Genesis 17:7–8 [God speaking to Abram], "I will establish My covenant between Me and you and your descendants after you throughout their generations for an everlasting covenant, to be God to you and to your descendants after you. I will give to you and to your descendants after you, the land of your sojournings, all the land of Canaan, for an everlasting possession; and I will be their God."

Part 1: Framing The Conversation

As I write this, in late May of 2024, it has been 232 days since Hamas's damnable incursion into Israel on October 7, 2023. During their terrorist raid, Hamas fighters killed more than 1,200 Israelis[1] and took as hostages more than 250 others. Some Christians respond, claiming that Israel has a right and even a necessity to defend itself. Others, like myself, while not denying that Israel has a right to protect itself,[2] cry out for an end to the violence and for a lasting peace to be enacted. After all, ending the war and establishing a lasting peace is genuinely in the best interest of everyone: Israelis and Palestinians.

Israel's response to Hamas's attack was quick and intense. Since October 7, Israel's assault on Gaza has left more than 35,000 dead and 75,000 wounded, and this does not include the thousands more missing and presumed dead under the rubble. The war on Gaza has also displaced—some multiple times—1.9 million people. As many as 17,000 children have become orphans, and countless others are now classified under the new acronym "WCNSF" (Wounded Child No Surviving Family). Israel's assault has crippled much of Gaza's infrastructure—including large-scale destruction of most of the housing units, businesses, every one of Gaza's twelve universities, and twenty-five of the thirty-six hospitals in the Gaza Strip. In addition, more than a thousand children have endured amputations without anesthesia, hundreds of women have suffered miscarriages, and, as I write, we are now beginning to see deaths from malnutrition and dehydration as a state of famine approaches the people of the Gaza Strip.

Numbers, however, do not tell the whole story. How does one quantify the lost hopes and dreams? I struggle to look at the photos of those who died—whether they be Israelis or Palestinians. Pictures of young people smiling and ready to tackle the world adorned in their graduation gowns; the wedding photos of

---

1. There are some questions about the number of Israelis that Hamas killed on October 7. This is because Israel acknowledges that IDF forces killed some of the 1,200+ Israelis who died. Nonetheless, Hamas is still responsible for the deaths of a significant number of Israelis.

2. The issue is undoubtedly much more complex than this.

Introduction

a young couple excited to share life together; and the images of young people full of vigor and ready to take on the world. I find it difficult—though necessary—to watch videos of children being pulled out of the rubble: some clinging desperately to a thread of life while others lie lifeless. Every picture represents a life that ended too soon. War does that.

Moreover, what about the intense trauma that will haunt the survivors—whether they be Israelis or Palestinians? Those who must live the rest of their lives with the memories of the loved ones now lost forever—memories of burying their child, spouse, sibling, or parent. I will never forget the video of two young children—a little boy of less than two years of age and his sister not older than four—as they sat on an examination table covered in dust with cuts all over their face and arms, presumably from the shrapnel of a recently exploded missile. The moment unfolds as, for no apparent reason, the little girl sweetly leans over and gently comforts her brother with a kiss on his cheek. However, as the camera pulls back, I am haunted by the image of these two young children shaking uncontrollably. Their trauma was so great that their body experienced neurogenic tremors. War does this also.

One would think that the church should be united on these convictions. After all, what can be more Christian than weeping with those who are weeping and crying out for an end to violence and war? The problem with the seemingly innocuous question, "What is the role of the church in all of this?" lies in the diversity of convictions regarding Israel. Why is this? How can this be? While various factors contribute to the diversity of opinions on the war on Gaza, one particular factor stands out: this conflict involves Israel.

WHAT IS THE ROLE OF THE CHURCH IN ALL THIS?

When it comes to Israel, Christians often find themselves firmly entrenched on one of two sides. On one side are Christian Zionists who contend that we must side with Israel. After all, what could be more apparent, they claim, than the fact that God promised Abraham (Abram) and his descendants that he would give the land to them and that he did so as "an everlasting covenant" (Gen 17:7) and "an everlasting possession" (Gen 17:8)? As a result, Christian Zionists assert that we must side with Israel. After all, the Scriptures are clear, "those who bless Israel will be blessed" (see Gen 12:1–3). For the Christian Zionist, Israel's assault on Gaza is nothing more than a justifiable act of self-defense against terrorists. On the other side are those who cry out for the rights of the Palestinians. For them, the attack of October 7, though damnable, did not happen in a vacuum. They claim that the only way to ensure that October 7 does not happen again is to obtain a lasting peace: one that assures Israel's security and the Palestinians' freedom.

The lines are drawn. On one side are those who assert that Israel has no choice but to eradicate Hamas, even if that means killing thousands of civilian noncombatants. For them, Christians must stand with Israel. On the other side are those who, while condemning Hamas's actions, especially those against civilians, plead for a just peace and an end to Israel's oppressive occupation.

For many Christians, there is no middle ground. Among the supporters of Israel, some, like Russell Moore, the editor of *Christianity Today*, claim, "'Bothsidesism' About Hamas Is a Moral Failure."[3] As a result, efforts to call for a just peace, one that benefits both Israelis and Palestinians, are met with accusations of siding with terrorists or the damning label of "antisemitism."[4]

What happens when historical events undermine our theological beliefs? How should we respond when we find ourselves so entrenched in a theological conviction that we become unable or unwilling to "weep with those who weep" (Rom 12:15) or to advocate for peace? Should such cognitive dissonance not invite us to reevaluate our convictions?

I hope that as Christians, we would, at the very least, reconsider our beliefs regarding war as an appropriate response to violence. While I do not deny that wars may sometimes be necessary,

3. See Moore, "'Bothsidesism' About Hamas Is a Moral Failure."
4. See discussion on "antisemitism" in chapter 10.

Introduction

I question whether or not the church should advocate for war. After all, as I will argue in the next chapter, violence is the way of the nations and not the way of Christ.[5] The present war in Gaza and the ongoing conflict is neither good for Israel nor the Palestinians.

---

5. This conviction is highlighted in my commentary *Revelation: A Love Story*.

2

CONTRASTING KINGDOMS

Rejoice with those who rejoice, and weep with those who weep (Rom 12:15).

Put your sword back into its place; for all those who take up the sword shall perish by the sword (Matt 26:52).

Evangelicals are the most dangerous people on the planet. We don't see them as either the hope of the world or irrelevant. They are a liability and we are committed to working around them (anonymous).[1]

Jesus wept (John 11:35).[2]

THE RAISING OF LAZARUS in John 11 presents one of the more fascinating stories in the Gospels. What is most puzzling is that Jesus

---

1. This statement came from a person who labors for peace and justice.
2. John 11:35 is often considered the shortest verse in the Bible. Technically 1 Thessalonians 5:16 ("rejoice always"; two words in the Greek text) is shorter in terms of word count. John 11:35 has three words in the Greek text—the word "the" precedes "Jesus").

seemed to be aware that the Father had called him to raise Lazarus from the dead. Jesus even affirms this when standing outside Lazarus's tomb; he says,

> *Father, I thank You that You have heard Me. I knew that You always hear Me; but because of the people standing around I said it, so that they may believe that You sent Me (John 11:42).*

Why, knowing that He would raise Lazarus from the dead, did Jesus weep (John 11:35)?

I believe that among the reasons why Jesus wept is that death is not what God intended. Things were not supposed to be this way. He was weeping at a world that included death and suffering.

NB: When I teach John 11, I like to add some brevity to the discussion by inquiring whether or not Lazarus had a say in his coming out of the tomb. Did he resist? Did he tell Jesus, "Nah, I'm good. I kind of like it here"?

We often assume that Jesus' miracles showcased his person and nature or resulted from compassion. While these may be true to an extent, I wonder if we should also understand Jesus' miracles, especially his healings, as glimpses into the nature of his kingdom. What if Jesus restored sight to people who lacked sight as a way of testifying that in his kingdom, there will be no blindness? What if he cured the sick to signify that in his kingdom, there will be an end to illness and suffering?

I want to suggest that recognizing the nature of the kingdom of God explains the significance of Jesus' acts and puts our mission into context. Moreover, I would like here to explore the mission of God's people and how it correlates to the kingdom of God.

UNDERSTANDING THE KING

The Christian mission is rooted in the nature of God. God called us to be his image bearers. I believe that being made in God's image entails a mission. It is a calling and a summons. We were made to rule in God's stead and in a way that makes him known—i.e., to image him (see Gen 1:26–27). Thus, Paul asserts,

> Be imitators of me, just as I also am of Christ (1 Cor 11:1).

To the Ephesians, he adds,

> Therefore be imitators of God (Eph 5:1).

If it is so that the mission of God's people is to make him known, then it behooves us both to know him and the nature of his kingdom within which God called us to rule so that we might carry forth his mission.

God is love

Christian mission begins with Jesus' exhortation,

> If anyone wishes to come after Me, he must deny himself, and take up his cross and follow Me (Mark 8:34).

In issuing this proclamation, Jesus calls his followers to a radical, self-denying, cross-bearing love for the sake of others. Such a love for the other does not merely reflect our commitment to Christ. It is also the way the world comes to know God. When we love, we make God known. After all, "God is love" (1 John 4:8).

When the followers of Christ love as God loves, that is, by laying down our lives for the other, we reflect Christ and his love for the world. This is what Jesus means when he declares,

> By this all men will know that you are My disciples, if you have love for one another" (John 13:35).

In other words, when we love one another, the world looks at us and concludes, "They must be Jesus people because they love the way Jesus loved."

Moreover, the Christian principle of loving others also extends to our enemies:

> But love your enemies, and do good, and lend, expecting nothing in return; and your reward will be great, and you will be sons of the Most High; for He Himself is kind to ungrateful and evil *men*" (Luke 6:35).

Once again, the implication is clear: When we love our enemies, we look like God because that is what He does!—as Jesus says, "for He Himself is kind to ungrateful and evil *men*" (Luke 6:35).

God is peace[3]

In addition, God is a god of peace. Consequently, Jesus declares that members of his kingdom pursue peace:

> Blessed are the peacemakers, for they shall be called sons of God (Matt 5:9).

When Jesus says that those who act as peacemakers will be called "sons of God,"[4] he is employing a figure of speech. In the ancient world, to be "a son of" something or someone implied reflecting the attributes and characteristics of that which one is a son of.[5] Consequently, when Jesus affirms peacemakers are blessed, it is because when we pursue peace, we are doing what God does.

God is just

That God commissions the people of God to do justice is abundantly evident throughout the Scriptures. The prophet Micah declares,

---

3. Although I will only present this thesis in brevity here, the notion that peace accompanies God's presence is central to the Scriptures. See Caynor, "Christ Our Peace."

4. The NET, NLT, and NRS read, "children of God." This is an acceptable translation in that blessedness is not restricted to men. The problem, however, is that it may obscure the figure of speech and the significance of being a "son of" in the ancient world.

5. Compare Jesus' accusation against the religious leaders who opposed Him: "You are of *your* father the devil, and you want to do the desires of your father" (John 8:44).

> He has told you, O man, what is good;
> And what does the Lord require of you
> But to do justice, to love kindness,
> And to walk humbly with your God? (Mic 6:8).

Isaiah similarly adds,

> Learn to do good;
> Seek justice,
> Reprove the ruthless,
> Defend the orphan,
> Plead for the widow (Isa 1:17).

Once again, we see that when the people of God pursue justice, we reflect the very nature of God:

> Righteousness and justice are the foundation of Your throne; Lovingkindness and truth go before You (Ps 89:14).

Consequently, loving our neighbors and even our enemies and pursuing peace and justice are rooted in the Christian commitment to imitate Christ and, thereby, make the Father known. Understanding our mission and the concomitant responsibility to make God known lies at the heart of the Christian calling to pursue peace and justice.

UNDERSTANDING THE KINGDOM

The Christian commitment to pursuing a just peace is also deeply rooted in a proper understanding of the kingdom of God. Perhaps one of the best ways of discerning the nature of the kingdom of God is to recognize the stark contrast between the kingdom of God and the kingdoms of the world.

The contrast between the two kingdoms[6] is evident in Jesus' affirmation to Pilate:

---

6. I say "two" kingdoms here to contrast Jesus' kingdom and the world's kingdoms—even though the latter comprises many kingdoms.

Contrasting Kingdoms

> My kingdom is not of this world. If My kingdom were of this world, then My servants would be fighting so that I would not be handed over to the Jews; but as it is, My kingdom is not of this realm (John 18:36).

This statement has been widely misunderstood in much of Western Christianity. Some have read Jesus' words as though he meant that his kingdom and the world's kingdoms operate in different realms: one in heaven and one on Earth. There is an element in which Jesus' kingdom is of a different realm. At the same time, it is evident that Jesus fully intends for his kingdom to conquer the kingdoms of the world. That is, his kingdom is not restricted to heaven.

Jesus' intention, however, appears to stress that the contrast between the kingdoms lies in the manner in which his kingdom operates when compared to the kingdoms of the world. This is why Jesus affirms, "If My kingdom were of this world, then My servants would be fighting" (John 18:36).

Consequently, Jesus' kingdom operates in a manner that is fundamentally at odds with how the world's kingdoms operate. Some of the disparities between the kingdom of God and the kingdoms of the world include:

- The kingdom of God recognizes that Jesus is the Lord.

  The kingdoms of the world profess allegiance to an array of other lords (e.g., Caesar, self, power, wealth, pleasure, comfort, empire).

- The kingdom of God is predicated on self-denial.

  The kingdoms of the world are predicated on self-satisfaction.

- The kingdom of God manifests itself in love for others, including one's enemies.

  The kingdoms of the world endeavor to dominate and, at times, destroy one's enemies.

- In the kingdom of God, power is expressed through love, epitomized by the cross.

  In the kingdoms of the world, power is often demonstrated by force, exemplified by placing people on crosses.

- The kingdom of God brings justice and peace to the world.

  The kingdoms of the world bring justice and peace to those in power, and they often do so by inflicting violence upon others.

- In the kingdom of God, the poor, the hungry, the meek, and the gentle are blessed.

  In the kingdoms of the world, those in power are often blessed at the expense of the poor and the marginalized.

Violence inflicted or violence endured?

Perhaps the most significant contrast for our interests between the kingdom of God and the kingdoms of the world pertains to power and the use of violence. As hinted at above, power in the kingdoms of the world is regularly demonstrated by inflicting violence. In contrast, power in the kingdom of God is manifested by suffering violence (cross-bearing love). One kingdom inflicts violence to maintain power, while the other suffers violence and demonstrates power through love.

A striking illustration of the contrasting use of power and violence occurs at Jesus' arrest. When the authorities arrive to arrest Jesus, he inquires, "Have you come out with swords and clubs to arrest Me?" (Matt 26:55). When his disciples respond to this show of force with a force of their own, Jesus rebukes them, demanding, "Put your sword back into its place; for all those who take up the sword shall perish by the sword" (Matt 26:52). For Jesus, the sword is what the nations use and, he declares, "This is not the way we do it in My kingdom."[7]

Interestingly, Jesus' disciples struggled to understand that his kingdom employed power in a fundamentally different manner from the kingdoms of the world. Thus, while journeying to Jerusalem, where the disciples reasonably assumed that Jesus would finally take his seat on the throne, James and John request of Jesus, "Grant that we may sit, one on Your right and one on *Your* left" (Mark 10:37). For James and John, it was a straightforward request. They wanted the two seats of power next to Jesus. The rest of the disciples, presumably because they wanted to have the seats of power themselves, were angered by James and John's request: "Hearing *this*, the ten began to feel indignant with James and John" (Mark 10:41). It is worth noting, however, that the only other instance of the expression "one on His right and one on His left" in the Gospel of Mark occurs in the description of the two thieves crucified next to Jesus, "one on His right and one on His left" (Mark 15:27). Thus, Jesus' reply to James and John, "You do not know what you are asking" (Mark 10:38). Jesus, speaking to the Twelve, elaborates once again on the contrastive nature of his kingdom compared to the kingdoms of the world:

> You know that those who are recognized as rulers of the Gentiles lord it over them; and their great men exercise authority over them. But it is not this way among you, but whoever wishes to become great among you shall be your servant; and whoever wishes to be first among you shall be slave of all. For even the Son of Man did not come to be served, but to serve, and to give His life a ransom for many (Mark 10:42–45).

With this contrast in mind, we return to Jesus' declaration to Pilate, "If My kingdom were of this world, then My servants would

---

7. In the book of Revelation, Jesus has a sword coming from His mouth, which signifies that his power is through the spoken word and not the use of the sword as a weapon of violence. Interestingly, in the book of Revelation, John uses two different words for sword, sometimes interchangeably. However, the word used for Jesus' sword and the word used for the sword of Rome are always distinguished. See my commentary *Revelation: A Love Story*.

be fighting" (John 18:36). In other words, Jesus affirms, "In My kingdom, we do not use violence, but love."

CONCLUSION

An essential feature of Christianity and the kingdom of God is that the people of God are to be fundamentally different from the world. After all, we follow a different King whose kingdom follows a different set of rules. To make our King known entails a call to a radical, self-denying, cross-bearing love for the other. We must love the way Jesus loved. But we must also pursue peace and justice.

3

UNDERSTANDING THE BIBLICAL NARRATIVE AND OUR ROLE IN IT

For God so loved the world . . . (John 3:16).

Then the King will say to those on His right, "Come, you who are blessed of My Father, inherit the kingdom prepared for you from the foundation of the world. For I was hungry, and you gave Me *something* to eat; I was thirsty, and you gave Me *something* to drink; I was a stranger, and you invited Me in; naked, and you clothed Me; I was sick, and you visited Me; I was in prison, and you came to Me." Then the righteous will answer Him, "Lord, when did we see You hungry, and feed You, or thirsty, and give You *something* to drink? And when did we see You a stranger, and invite You in, or naked, and clothe You? When did we see You sick, or in prison, and come to You?" The King will answer and say to them, "Truly I say to you, to the extent that you did it to one of these brothers of Mine, *even* the least *of them,* you did it to Me" (Matt 25:34–40).

Part 1: Framing The Conversation

SEVERAL YEARS AGO, I was meditating on the Lord's Prayer when I had an epiphany. For years (I am almost embarrassed to admit this, but here goes), I had uttered the line, "Thy kingdom come," thinking that in saying it, I was somehow giving God permission to do his will—as if he needed my permission. It was as if I was saying, "Come on, Lord, what are you waiting for?" At that moment, I suddenly realized that this is not what this part of the prayer means. Instead, when we pray, "Thy kingdom come," we are affirming our availability for God to do his work through us. We are acknowledging, "Here I am, Lord. I am available."

It is an important truth: God builds his kingdom through us. He uses us to do the work of his kingdom. I often like to ask my students, "Where was Paul when he experienced his transformation?" (I do not think "conversion" is the correct word.) Inevitably, someone will say, "On the road to Damascus." I then point out that God blinded Paul on the road to Damascus, and we do not usually associate blindness with transformation. Instead, I assert that Paul's transformation occurred in Damascus after Ananias laid hands on him. God may have intervened and blinded Paul. However, he used Ananias to open Paul's eyes.

During a recent trip with a good friend, our conversation shifted to address a Christian pastor we both knew. This pastor had caused considerable harm to many. With a measure of anguish, my friend turned to me and said, "Rob, why did God allow him to remain in power and continue to hurt so many? Why didn't God take him out?" I understood his sentiment. I, too, wished God would have acted. However, I replied that I was not sure it was God's fault. After all, I said, "God tried to have him removed. He tried to get him the help he needed." Then I noted, "The Lord put this person (I will not name names here), and this person, and this person, and this person in positions of power to remove the pastor from office and to get him the help he needed. The problem was that they all failed to do their job."

This is how God operates. He calls us to do the work of his kingdom. "Thy kingdom come."

UNDERSTANDING THE BIBLICAL NARRATIVE

I believe the Bible—from Genesis through Revelation—tells a grand narrative. And I believe that narrative is a love story.[1] One of the central features of this love story relates to God's desire to dwell among all humanity and throughout the entirety of the creation.

Tragically, as with all good stories, a plot twist enters the biblical account on page three. Instead of choosing to acknowledge God (YHWH) and his infinite wisdom as the basis for discerning right and wrong, humanity (Adam and Eve) decided that they will determine right and wrong for themselves. Instead of dwelling in God's garden presence and fulfilling the divine mission of making God known (i.e., being his image bearers) to the creation, humanity is expelled from God's presence.

God, in his great love, however, does not abandon humanity. Instead, he chooses a man—Abraham—and his descendants. They will be his *people*. And it will be among them that God will dwell. In addition, it is through them that God would make himself known to the nations. In other words, God did not choose Abraham and his descendants merely for their own sake. Instead, He chose them for a purpose: to be a blessing to the nations:

> And in you all the families of the earth will be blessed (Gen 12:3).

Moreover, as the covenant people, Abraham and his descendants were to inherit the land designated for them. This land would be the *place* where God will dwell among them. The covenant formula in Leviticus 26 expresses the heart of the covenant promise:

> Moreover, I will make My dwelling among you, and My soul will not reject you. I will also walk among you and be your God, and you shall be My people (Lev 26:11–12).

As the biblical story proceeds, however, Abraham and his descendants, like Adam and Eve before them, fail to be faithful to their missional calling. Consequently, like Adam and Eve, they are

---

1. See my commentary *Revelation: A Love Story*, where I argue that even the book of Revelation is a love story.

driven from the land. First, the Assyrians banish the ten northern tribes of Israel. Then the Babylonians expel the southern tribes of Judah. All hope appears lost at this point in the story. The descendants of Abraham have been expelled from the place where God dwelt among them and from which they were to make God known to the nations. Moreover, as Isaiah affirms, they do not even know the Lord themselves:

> Sons I have reared and brought up,
> But they have revolted against Me.
> An ox knows its owner,
> And a donkey its master's manger,
> *But* Israel does not know,
> My people do not understand (Isa 1:2–3).

It is here that Ezekiel enters the story. The Lord reveals to the prophet[2] that he will restore them to the land:

> And they will be My people, and I will be their God. My servant David will be king over them, and they will all have one shepherd; and they will walk in My ordinances and keep My statutes and observe them. They will live on the land that I gave to Jacob My servant, in which your fathers lived; and they will live on it, they, and their sons and their sons' sons, forever; and David My servant will be their prince forever. And I will place them and multiply them, and will set My sanctuary in their midst forever. My dwelling place also will be with them; and I will be their God, and they will be My people (Ezek 37:23b–27).

It is critical to observe that when Ezekiel assures them of God's restoration as a people and to the land, he explicitly references the covenant formula of Leviticus 26:12–13. He asserts both, I "will set My sanctuary in their midst forever" (Ezek 37:26; see Lev 26:11), and "I will be their God, and they will be My people" (Ezek 37:27; see Lev 26:12).

---

2. Ezekiel was formerly a priest and later commissioned as a prophet (Ezek 1:3).

Understanding the Biblical Narrative and Our Role in It

The Old Testament story, therefore, ends with this hope. The hope that someday, God will restore his people to the land and he dwell among them. In doing so, he will also enable his people to fulfill their mission of making him known to the nations.

With this understanding of the Old Testament story in view, the question for our purposes becomes twofold.

- First, does the New Testament indicate that Jesus fulfilled the mission God called Abraham and his descendants to accomplish? And, if so, does the New Testament expand the identity of the chosen people to include all those who have faith in him?

- Second, does the promise of land still apply to the physical descendants of Abraham, or has the promise of land also been fulfilled by Jesus and, through the Spirit, the New Testament people of God? And, if so, does the New Testament expand the land to include everywhere the Spirit-filled people of God are?

CONCLUSION

In part two of this work, I will contend that the restoration of both the people of God and the land of promise begins with the coming of Jesus. He is the one through whom God accomplishes his purposes. What God called Abraham and his descendants (and Adam and Eve before them) to do, God, in the person of Christ, did. As Paul affirms,

> For as many as are the promises of God, in Him they are yes (2 Cor 1:20).

The biblical story, then, is one in which God himself enters the scene and does for humanity what humanity was not able to do for itself.[3]

---

3. It should be noted that Abraham and his descendants could not fulfill their missional call because they descended from Adam and Eve. What was needed was for God himself to enter the story and do for humanity what

Part 1: Framing The Conversation

The biblical story, of course, does not end with Jesus. The New Testament story continues as Jesus sends his Spirit to dwell within his people. As a result, the Spirit-filled followers of Christ carry forth the missional call of making God known to the nations. Moreover, they do so as the people of God among whom God dwells. This story climaxes in the new Jerusalem, where all the nations[4] inhabit the city of God and where God himself dwells among them.

---

humanity could not do for itself.

4. I do not intend to suggest that everyone is saved, only that people from every nation inhabit the new Jerusalem.

PART 2

A BIBLICAL THEOLOGY OF THE TEMPLE, THE PEOPLE, AND THE LAND

4

THE BIBLICAL NARRATIVE AND THE TEMPLE

Now when these things have been so prepared, the priests are continually entering the outer tabernacle performing the divine worship, but into the second, only the high priest enters once a year, not without taking blood, which he offers for himself and for the sins of the people committed in ignorance (Heb 9:6–7).

And one called out to another and said, "Holy, Holy, Holy, is the Lord of hosts, the whole earth is full of His glory" (Isa 6:3).

ANY DISCUSSION RELATING TO the promises of family (as numerous as the stars; Gen 15:5; 22:17) and land to Abraham must begin with understanding the temple and its role in the biblical narrative. This is because the promises to Abraham and his descendants cannot be divorced from the fact that God chose Abraham and his descendants to be the *people* among whom God would dwell, and the land was to be the *place* where God would dwell among them. Consequently, the temple is central to the biblical story.

Part 2: A Biblical Theology of The Temple, The People, and The Land

It must be noted, however, that God did not desire for his presence to dwell in one place and among one people. Instead, as the new Jerusalem reveals (Rev 21:9–22:9), God desired to dwell with all people and throughout the entirety of the creation.

After Adam and Eve were expelled from God's presence in the garden, the story turns to God's eventual choosing of Abraham and his descendants. As I alluded to previously, they were not chosen for their own sake. Instead, they were to manifest the divine image to the nations and thereby bring the nations into his covenant community. As a result, "The whole earth is full of His glory" (Isa 6:3).

Since Jesus was God among us, there is little doubt that by its very nature, he himself is the temple presence of God.

That this is narrative trajectory of the biblical story is evident throughout the Scriptures. It is most apparent, however, in the fulfillment that occurs in the new Jerusalem. In the new Jerusalem, the covenant promises are reiterated:

> The voice declares, "Behold the dwelling place of God is with mankind, and He will dwell with them, and they themselves will be His people, and God Himself will be with them" (Rev 21:3).

Reference to the covenantal promise also occurs in Rev 21:7, where the one seated on the throne says,

> I will be God to him and he himself will be my son (Rev 21:7).

What is critical for understanding the biblical narrative, however, is that as long as the covenant people ("Israel") remained a distinct entity from the nations and as long as the land remained a distinct piece of real estate, God's presence would remain limited to one people and one place. In other words, Israel could never have fulfilled the covenant promises alone. Thus, God always intended for the promises of family and land to extend to the nations.

The Biblical Narrative and the Temple

THE TEMPLE'S ROLE IN THE BIBLICAL NARRATIVE

The presence of God among his people figures prominently in the biblical story. As I noted in the opening of this chapter, two vital elements of God's temple presence include God's desire to dwell among all people and throughout the entirety of the creation.[1] What was lost, then, with the entrance of sin into the biblical story and the subsequent expulsion of Adam and Eve from the garden of Eden, was the divine presence among humanity. In Eden, God "walked" in the midst of humanity (Gen 3:8).

After the banishing of Adam and Eve, God occasionally manifests his presence to the patriarchs. Later, he permits Moses and the Israelites to erect a tabernacle. Eventually, he instructs Solomon to build a more permanent dwelling place for him (a temple). At this juncture of the narrative, God's dwelling among his people remained limited to one person and one place. In other words, this was not the ideal. As a result, God's dwelling in a temple made by human hands was only a temporary provision.

The nature and purpose of the temple

It is not uncommon for some modern Christian prophetic pundits to contend that a physical temple (a third temple) must be built in Jerusalem before Christ's return. This supposition is often buttressed by an abundance of citations of (Old Testament) prophecies that, it is asserted, have yet to be fulfilled.

There are two significant problems with this conviction. First, the notion that a third temple will be built in fulfillment of the covenant promises fails to account for the very nature and purpose of the temple and its role in the covenant. Namely, the temple represents the place where God would dwell among his people. Second, the suggestion that a third temple will be rebuilt in fulfillment of

---

1. See my *Understanding the New Testament and the End Times* and *These Brothers of Mine: A Biblical Theology of Land and Family and a Response to Christian Zionism*.

the covenant promises to Israel ignores the New Testament's affirmation that Jesus fulfills all of God's promises:

> For the Son of God, Christ Jesus, who was preached among you by us—by me and Silvanus and Timothy—was not yes and no, but is yes in Him. For as many as are the promises of God, in Him they are yes; therefore also through Him is our Amen to the glory of God through us (2 Cor 1:19–20).

That this includes the promise of a restored temple is explicit in the declaration that Jesus is the temple of God in John 2:

> Jesus answered them, "Destroy this temple, and in three days I will raise it up." The Jews then said, "It took forty-six years to build this temple, and will You raise it up in three days?" But He was speaking of the temple of His body (John 2:19–21).

God's temple is wherever he resides

Throughout much of the Old Testament narrative, the tabernacle of Moses and later the temple serve as the location of God's presence among his people. At the same time, we know that God's nature transcends the confines of a physical building. Stephen argues this point in his famed discourse in Acts 7. He observes that God appeared to Abraham in Mesopotamia (Acts 7:2) and Moses in the wilderness (Acts 7:30–34). Stephen's point is that God appeared in both instances before the tabernacle was erected and outside the land.

That God transcends the confines of a building is also affirmed by Solomon's dedicatory speech after the completion of the temple construction: "Behold, heaven and the highest heaven cannot contain You, how much less this house which I have built" (1 Kgs 8:27). In the New Testament, Paul takes this principle one step further when he declares to the Athenians, "The God who made the world and all things in it, since He is Lord of heaven and earth, does not dwell in temples made with hands" (Acts 17:24; see 7:48).

That God's presence transcends the confines of a physical building, of course, does not preclude the fact that for a time he chose to dwell within the tabernacle of Moses and the temple of Solomon.

It is also essential to understand that the tabernacle of Moses and the later temple placed two fundamental limitations on God's presence. First, such physical structures limited God's presence to one place. Second, they restricted God's presence to only one person—the high priest, who alone was permitted into the holy of holies and only once per year.

The covenant promise

God enters into a covenant with Abraham and his descendants, promising they will become his people and he will be their God. The covenant includes blessings for obedience and curses for disobedience, as outlined in Deuteronomy 27–30 and Leviticus 26. At the close of the covenant blessings in Leviticus 26:1–13, we find the stipulation that God desires to dwell among them:

> Moreover, I will make My dwelling among you, and My soul will not reject you. I will also walk among you and be your God, and you shall be My people (Lev 26:11–12).

It is critical to observe that this covenant promise that God would dwell among his people echoes the creation account. Just as God "walked" in the garden of Eden (Gen 3:8), so he will again "walk among you" (Lev 26:12).

Following the temple's destruction in 586 BCE, the latter prophets emerge with the assurance that God would again restore his presence among the people. The prophet Ezekiel, for example, emphasizes that God will again make a covenant with his people, which will incorporate the restoration of God's presence among his people:

> I will make a covenant of peace with them; it will be an everlasting covenant with them. And I will place them and multiply them, and will set My sanctuary in their midst forever. My dwelling place also will be with them;

and I will be their God, and they will be My people (Ezek 37:26–27).

As noted in the previous chapter, it is critical to recognize that Ezekiel's assurance that God will restore the temple reiterates the language of Leviticus 26:11–12. The restoration, in other words, will occur in accordance with the covenant promise and the restoration of Eden.

Consequently, discussions related to the promises to Abraham and his descendants—both that they will be as numerous as the stars and they will inherit the land—must be understood in light of the temple and the promise of restoration found in the latter prophets such as Ezekiel.

The question for us today is whether or not Jesus fulfilled these promises or if they await a future restoration of the physical descendants of Abraham to the land. There is little question in my mind that the New Testament affirms that Jesus is the temple of God and that he is so in accordance with the promises of restoration as found in Ezekiel.[2]

JESUS AS THE TEMPLE

When we turn to the pages of the New Testament, we recognize that Jesus himself, in the flesh, represents the temple presence of God. This is evident in the Gospel of John's opening prologue (John 1:1–18). John begins his prologue by affirming that Jesus is the manifestation of God:

> In the beginning was the Word, and the Word was with God, and the Word was God. He was in the beginning with God. All things came into being through Him, and apart from Him nothing came into being that has come into being (John 1:1–3).

---

2. Some Christian Zionists might agree that Jesus is the temple and still contend that the promises remain applicable to the ethnic descendants of Abraham.

It is noteworthy that John's opening phrase, "In the beginning," establishes an unmistakable connection with the creation account in Genesis.

As John continues, he also associates the incarnation of Jesus with the temple presence of God:

> And the Word became flesh, and dwelt among us (John 1:14).

John's use of "dwelt" in John 1:14 is the verbal form of the noun often used to denote the tabernacle of Moses. Thus, John declares that Jesus is not only God in the flesh but that he is the God who dwelt in the temple. The connection with the temple presence of God is further established when John adds,

> And we saw His glory (John 1:14).

That Jesus is temple presence of God is evident in that the glory of God (John 1:14) is regularly associated with the presence of God. For example,

> It happened that when the priests came from the holy place, the cloud filled the house of the Lord, so that the priests could not stand to minister because of the cloud, for the glory of the Lord filled the house of the Lord (1 Kgs 8:10–11).

And,

> And the glory of the Lord came into the house by the way of the gate facing toward the east. And the Spirit lifted me up and brought me into the inner court; and behold, the glory of the Lord filled the house (Ezek 43:4–5).

As noted earlier, in John 2:18–21, Jesus explicitly declares that he is the temple of God:

> Jesus answered them, "Destroy this temple, and in three days I will raise it up." The Jews then said, "It took forty-six years to build this temple, and will You raise it up in three days?" But He was speaking of the temple of His body (John 2:19–21).

Therefore, John's prologue announces that the glorious presence of God, which once dwelt in the tabernacle and later the temple, now walked among them in the person of Christ! John's use of "we" in the phrase "we saw His glory" (John 1:14) cannot be overlooked. By using "we," John declares that more than one person has now encountered the presence of God. Thus, whereas the Old Testament temple presence of God was restricted to one person and only once per year, the temple presence of God was now experienced by many people. That is, the temple presence of God has expanded in that more than one person now experiences the presence of God.

The question remains as to whether or not Jesus is the temple in fulfillment of God's promise to restore his temple presence among his people.

THE TEMPLE EXPANDED: THE CHURCH AS GOD'S DWELLING PLACE

As we venture into the epistles of the New Testament, we see that the temple presence of God expands further through the Spirit's indwelling of the people of God. Because the Spirit dwells within the people of God, the New Testament affirms that they become the place of God's presence—i.e., the temple. In fact, for Paul, Jesus is now the "cornerstone" (Eph 2:20), and the New Testament people of God are the temple:

> So then you are no longer strangers and aliens, but you are fellow citizens with the saints, and are of God's household, having been built on the foundation of the apostles and prophets, Christ Jesus Himself being the corner *stone*, in whom the whole building, being fitted together, is growing into a holy temple in the Lord, in whom you also are being built together into a dwelling of God in the Spirit (Eph 2:19–22).

That the entirety of the people of God has become the place of God's temple presence is also evident in Paul's declaration to the Corinthians. Paul associates the people of God in Corinth both with garden imagery that surely relates them with Eden and with the temple:

> I planted, Apollos watered, but God was causing the growth. So then neither the one who plants nor the one who waters is anything, but God who causes the growth. Now he who plants and he who waters are one; but each will receive his own reward according to his own labor (1 Cor 3:6–8).

After associating the beginning of the church in Corinth with the planting of a garden, Paul immediately follows this by associating them with a building:

> For we are God's fellow workers; you are God's field, God's building (1 Cor 3:9).

The Christ-followers in Corinth, however, are not merely a building; they are themselves the temple of God:

> Do you not know that you are a temple of God, and *that* the Spirit of God dwells in you? (1 Cor 3:16).

Later, in 2 Corinthians, Paul reiterates that the Christ-followers in Corinth are the temple of God:

> For we are the temple of the living God; just as God said, "I will dwell in them and walk among them; And I will be their God, and they shall be My people" (2 Cor 6:16).

It is critical to recognize that when Paul affirms that the Christ-followers in Corinth have become the temple presence of God, he does so by citing covenant promise of Leviticus 26:12–13, "They shall be My people" (2 Cor 6:16), and the promise of a restored temple in Ezekiel 37:26–27, "I will dwell in them and walk among them; And I will be their God" (2 Cor 6:16).

This is of paramount importance. As iterated in Leviticus, the covenant promises to Abraham and his descendants that they would be his people and that God would dwell among them are fulfilled through the indwelling of the Spirit within the Christ-followers in Corinth.

Not only is the presence of God within the New Testament people of God identified as the fulfillment of the covenant promises given to the Old Testament people of God and in fulfillment of the promise of the restoration, but the fulfillment also corresponds to the thesis that God desired to dwell among his people and to extend his presence among all people and throughout the whole of creation. We have seen that with the incarnation of Christ, the temple presence of God has begun to expand so that more than one person beheld the "glory" of God ("we saw His glory," John 1:14). Now, by means of the Spirit's indwelling the New Testament people of God, God's temple presence is experienced by more and more people. Furthermore, as the gospel spreads throughout the world, God's temple presence also extends throughout the world. God's presence is experienced by more people and in more places. Thus, the fulfillment of God's desire to dwell among all people and throughout the creation is unfolding.

THE ULTIMATE FULFILLMENT OF GOD'S PRESENCE: THE NEW JERUSALEM

The ultimate fulfillment of God's desire to dwell among all people and throughout the creation occurs in the new Jerusalem (Rev 21–22). What is significant for us is that John's opening description of the new Jerusalem cites the covenant promises of Leviticus and Ezekiel. First, John hears,

> Behold, the tabernacle of God is among men, and He will dwell among them, and they shall be His people, and God Himself will be among them (Rev 21:3).

Then the Father, who sits on the throne, adds,

> He who overcomes will inherit these things, and I will be his God and he will be My son" (Rev 21:7).

It is evident then that the consummation of the covenant promise that God would dwell among His people, as described in Leviticus 26:11–12 and in the hope of restoration described in Ezekiel

37:26–27, arrives with the new Jerusalem. What we will see in the following chapters is that the new Jerusalem is not simply a temple-city but that it represents the people of God (the Bride) dwelling eternally in the presence of God and that it fills the entirety of the new creation.

CONCLUSION

In the following two chapters, we will delve into the questions about the choosing of Abraham and his descendants (people) and the promise of land given to them. I will contend that the promises relating to the people and the land cannot be divorced from the larger biblical narrative and God's desire to dwell among all people and throughout his creation.

5

THE BIBLICAL NARRATIVE AND THE PEOPLE OF GOD

And He took him outside and said, "Now look toward the heavens, and count the stars, if you are able to count them." And He said to him, "So shall your descendants be" (Gen 15:5).

... indeed I will greatly bless you, and I will greatly multiply your seed as the stars of the heavens and as the sand which is on the seashore (Gen 22:17).

SEVERAL YEARS AGO, I began a sermon by saying, "This is going to sound like blasphemy." I assured the congregation it was not blasphemy, at least I did not think it was. I proceeded to assert, "Jesus did not finish the job." Admittedly, that sure sounds blasphemous. The problem is that we have defined "the job" as, "dying on the cross, atoning for sin, and rising from the dead." Of course, if that is what the job is, then Jesus indeed finished the job. But what if "the job" also entailed faithfully carrying forth the mission of God's people of making God known to the nations? If this is a part of "the job," then Jesus did not finish it.

In John 12, there is an interesting scene that, at first glance, does not make much sense. Jesus enters Jerusalem. His passion is close at hand. John then adds that some Greeks—likely Greek-speaking or Hellenistic Jews[1]—were also in town for the Passover. The Greeks then approach Philip—the only disciple of Jesus with a Greek name—and ask, "Sir, we wish to see Jesus" (John 12:20). Philip and Andrew then relay the message to Jesus. Jesus' reply appears to have nothing to do with the simple request for some Greek-speaking Jews to see him:

> *The hour has come for the Son of Man to be glorified. Truly, truly, I say to you, unless a grain of wheat falls into the earth and dies, it remains alone; but if it dies, it bears much fruit (John 12:23–24).*

You almost have to wonder if the disciples were thinking, "Um, that is great, Jesus, but these dudes just want to know if they can stop by for a quick 'Hello.'" What does Jesus' waxing eloquently about wheat falling to the ground have to do with their request? It actually has everything to do with their request to see Jesus.

Why is it that the approach of the Greeks was an indication that Jesus' hour had come? The answer is that for Jesus, the approaching of Hellenistic Jews was a sign that the time for his death had arrived; or, as the Gospel of John puts it, "The hour has come" (John 13:1). In other words, the mission to the nations was for the disciples and the early Christ-followers to accomplish. Therefore, for Jesus, the arrival of the Hellenists indicated that it was time for the grain of wheat to die and rise again.

Discussions about "Who are the people of God?" often get bogged down in prooftexting. On the one hand, the Christian Zionists—who contend that the promises to Abraham and his descendants

---

1. See John 7:35. They were from the "dispersion." The fact that they were in town for the Passover certainly indicates that they are Greek speaking, or Hellenistic, Jews. See also Acts 6:1–6. Hellenistic Jews are, among other things, Jews who live outside the land, speak Greek (predominately), and have adopted other elements of the Greco-Roman culture. However, they identify as Jews, as evidenced by their attending Jerusalem for the feast.

Part 2: A Biblical Theology of The Temple, The People, and The Land

apply only to the physical descendants of Abraham—have a vast array of Old Testament verses to confirm that the promises to Abraham apply only to the physical descendants of Abraham. On the other hand, the non-Zionist Christian, like myself—who contend that in the New Testament, Jesus and the people of God (i.e., the church)[2] fulfill the promises to Abraham—have our own arsenal of verses from the New Testament to confirm that the promises to Abraham and his descendants are fulfilled first by Jesus and then by the New Testament people of God (the church). While one side proclaims that the Old Testament is explicit, the other side asserts that the New Testament is equally explicit.[3] One side claims to read the Old Testament in light of itself. The other side declares that the New Testament reads the Old Testament in light of Jesus, and so should we.

I contend that what is missing from these debates is an effort to discern the purpose for which God called Abraham and his descendants. After all, it is one thing to argue whether or not the Old Testament people of God remain distinct from the New Testament people of God. However, it is another thing to discern why God

2. I prefer the title "the people of God" because it suggests continuity between the Old Testament people of God and the New Testament people of God. Employing the terms "Israel" and "the church" tends to facilitate an understanding that they are two distinct groups. Those who believe that the promises to Abraham and his descendants, including the promise of land, still apply to the Jewish people, often assert that the Jewish people ("Israel") represent the physical people of God and "the church" are the spiritual people of God. Although addressing this point will take us too far afield, it cannot go without saying that the biblical writers did not think in terms of a radical distinction between the physical and the spiritual. Such distinctions are attributed to Platonic (or Epicurean) thinking and do not enter Christian history until after the New Testament era.

3. This is not to say that Christian Zionists do not cite New Testament verses in support of their position or that non-Zionist Christians do not have Old Testament verses that they will cite. The question is, are the New Testament writers reading the Old Testament and the covenant promises in light of Jesus or strictly in light of the Old Testament context? I will not address the questions in this manner. Instead, I will contend that the New Testament writers find the fulfillment of the Old Testament covenant promises in Jesus. Whether this fulfillment constitutes a rereading of the Old Testament extends beyond the scope of this study.

called Abraham and his descendants. The reason why I believe that this is a critical question is because it offers another means of identifying the people of God. With this in mind, I will contend that the followers of Christ (aka, "the New Testament people of God" or "the church") are not merely given the same titles/designations as the Old Testament people of God (Israel). They also carry out the mission of God's people. If this is so, then the New Testament people of God are the descendants of Abraham because they fulfill the mission for which God chose Abraham and his descendants.

THE MISSION OF GOD'S PEOPLE

Understanding the purpose for which God called Abraham begins with discerning humanity's role in the creation narrative and how Abraham and his descendants were entrusted with a mission. Foremost among the roles of humanity was the designation of God's image bearers (Gen 1:26). As the bearers of God's image, humanity was to reflect God's nature to the creation and thereby make him known. God's image bearers also enjoyed the presence of God, who walked among them (Gen 3:8).[4]

This intimate fellowship with God was among the things lost when God expelled Adam and Eve from the garden.[5] In addition, humanity's mission of making God known became more difficult. For one, humanity was no longer unified—as evidenced by their recognition of their nakedness (Gen 3:7). Thus, their ruling over the creation would now be fraught with conflict. In addition, the missional call to make God known includes the necessity of making him known to the rest of humanity.

---

4. An incidental but not insignificant detail is that in the second creation account in Genesis 2, Adam was not made in the garden but outside of it (see Gen 2:8; 3:23).

5. Note that the curse and subsequent expulsion from the garden did not negate the commands to Adam and Eve to be "fruitful and multiply," nor to "rule" and "subdue" the Earth, nor to "cultivate" and "keep." Instead, the curse and expulsion meant that fulfilling these duties would be more difficult (see Gen 3:17–19).

It is here that Abraham and his descendants enter the story. God chooses Abraham[6] and promises to be with him and to bless him and his "descendants/offspring/seed" (Gen 26:3).[7] Included in the promise of blessing was the responsibility for them to be a source of blessing to the nations:

> Now the LORD said to Abram, "Go forth from your country, And from your relatives And from your father's house, To the land which I will show you; And I will make you a great nation, And I will bless you, And make your name great; And so you shall be a blessing; And I will bless those who bless you, And the one who curses you I will curse. And in you all the families of the earth will be blessed" (Gen 12:1–3).

Isaiah explicitly affirms that the Old Testament people of God were called to make God known to the nations:

> I will appoint You as a covenant to the people,
> As a light to the nations (Isa 42:6).

Isaiah 49 reiterates the task:

> I will also make You a light of the nations
> So that My salvation may reach to the end of the earth
> (Isa 49:6).

Recognizing that God called Abraham and his descendants, not simply for their own sake, but also that they might be a blessing to "all the families of the earth" (Gen 12:3), is critical when it comes to discerning the identity of the people of God. When we read the promises made to the Old Testament people of God in light of the fact that they were to be the people among whom God would dwell and in light of their mission to make him known, it becomes evident that the promises begin to find their fulfillment in Jesus.

---

6. At the time, he was known as "Abram."

7. See Gen 12:7; Gen 13:15; 15:5; 17:7; 22:17–18: The NAS varies between "descendants" and "seed"; the NET, NLT, and NKJ read, "descendants"; the ESV says, "offspring"—with a footnote adding "seed"; the NIV and NRS vary between "descendants" and "offspring."

The Biblical Narrative and The People of God

JESUS IS THE FULFILLMENT OF THE PEOPLE OF GOD

The New Testament abundantly affirms that Jesus embodies the identity of the people of God. That he does so is evidenced by the fact that every significant title associated with the Old Testament people of God (Israel) is ascribed to Jesus. Thus, Jesus is the true Adam (1 Cor 15:45). He is the "Son of God" (Mark 1:1; Luke 3:38).[8] He is the "Firstborn son of God" (Heb 1:6; Rom 8:29; Col 1:15, 18; see Exod 4:22; Hos 11:1). He is the prophet who is like Moses and yet is greater than Moses (Acts 3:22; Heb 3:1–6). He is the true high priest (Heb 4:14). He is the true king of Israel (Acts 2:22–36).

That Jesus embodies the people of God in fulfillment of the promises to Abraham is made explicit in Paul's identification of Jesus with the promised "seed" of Abraham:

> Now the promises were spoken to Abraham and to his seed. He does not say, "And to seeds," as *referring* to many, but *rather* to one, "And to your seed," that is, Christ (Gal 3:16).[9]

Thus, the New Testament portrays Jesus as the true humanity in continuity with Adam, Abraham, and the Old Testament people of God. At this point, Christian Zionists may well agree that Jesus is identified with the Old Testament people of God (Israel). Nonetheless, they claim that the promises to Abraham and his descendants still apply to the ethnic descendants of Abraham.

This brings me to my second point. Jesus is not merely the true "seed" of Abraham, but he also accomplishes the very purpose for which God called Abraham and his descendants—namely, to be a light to the nations. That Jesus carries forth the mission to which God chose Abraham and his descendants is evident in the Gospel of Luke. In Luke 2, Joseph and Mary bring the newborn Jesus to the temple. An old man named Simeon was residing in Jerusalem at the time. God promised Simeon that he would not die

---

8. Contrary to popular opinion, this title does not convey the notion of Jesus' deity but, corresponding with the previous title, expresses his humanity.

9. Compare with Genesis 22:17–18.

until he saw the Christ (Luke 2:26). Upon seeing the child, Simeon declares that he can now "depart in peace" (Luke 2:29). He then affirms,

> For my eyes have seen Your salvation,
> Which You have prepared in the presence of all peoples,
> A Light of revelation to the Gentiles,
> And the glory of Your people Israel (Luke 2:30–32).

It is critical to observe that Simeon identifies Jesus as the promised Christ because he came to do what God had called Israel to do. Simeon cites Israel's mission expressed in Isaiah 42:6 and 49:6 and acknowledges that Jesus is the Christ because this is what he came to do.

The Gospel of John also affirms that Jesus fulfills the mission of God's people. There Jesus explicitly declares, "I am the light of the world" (John 8:12; 9:5). Similarly, the book of Revelation identifies Jesus in accord with the mission of Israel. Thus, Jesus is the "faithful witness" (Rev 1:5; 3:14).[10]

Therefore, the New Testament identifies Jesus both as the embodiment of the people of God (Israel) and as the one who accomplishes the very purpose for which Abraham and his descendants were called.[11]

---

10. It is worth noting that of all the accolades given to Jesus in the book of Revelation, "faithful witness" (Rev 1:5) is the first.

11. The reasoning I have presented here is more conclusive than many responses to the arguments presented by Christian Zionists. Most non-Zionist Christians center the debate around whether or not the New Testament applies to Jesus the titles and attributes that belong to Israel. Even though Jesus undoubtedly has such titles and attributes, the Christian Zionist rejoinder is that the promises remain applicable to the physical descendants of Abraham. However, if, as I am setting forth, Jesus is not merely the representative descendant of Abraham, but he also fulfills the very purpose for which Abraham and his descendants were called. Consequently, the notion that the promises remain applicable to the Jewish people has been dealt a death blow. After all, what purpose would there be for restoring the ethnic descendants of Abraham? The mission has been fulfilled. In Jesus and, as I will contend below, the Spirit's indwelling of the New Testament people of God, the fulfillment of the promises has begun. To contend that there must be a restoration of an ethnically identifiable people would be to move the fulfillment backward.

THROUGH THE SPIRIT, THE FULFILLMENT OF THE PEOPLE OF GOD CONTINUES BY MEANS OF THE NEW TESTAMENT PEOPLE OF GOD

Jesus inaugurates the mission of making God known to the nations, which was first given to Abraham and his descendants. However, this mission is not consummated until the descent of the new Jerusalem. In the present the mission continues in the lives of the New Testament people of God through the indwelling of the Spirit.

Every major title and attribute for Israel is applied to the New Testament people of God (i.e., the church)

Like Jesus, the New Testament depicts the people of God (the church) in continuity with the Old Testament people of God (Israel). This is evident in that virtually every major title and attribute of Israel is applied to the followers of Christ in the New Testament.

This is particularly evident in 1 Peter. Peter affirms that the Christ-followers to whom he writes are "A chosen race, a royal priesthood, a holy nation, a people for *God's* own possession" (1 Pet 2:9).[12] That the Christ-followers are "chosen" corresponds with the designation given to Israel in Isaiah 43:20. That they are a "royal priesthood" and "holy" links them with the Israelites who escaped from Egypt in Exodus 19:5. That they are a "people for God's own possession" corresponds with the designation of Israel in Exodus 19:5, Isaiah 43:21, and Malachi 3:17.[13]

---

12. It is sometimes suggested that Peter wrote to Jewish Christians. The text of 1 Peter suggests they come from a pagan background. For example, Peter exhorts his readers, "Do not be conformed to the former lusts *which were yours* in your ignorance" (1 Pet 1:14). It is doubtful that Peter would refer to Jewish followers of Christ as previously being in "ignorance." See also 1 Peter 4:1–4, where Peter refers to his readers as those who in the past "carried out the desires of the Gentiles" (1 Pet 4:3).

13. Note that 1 Pet 2:4–10 also applies the same titles for Jesus and the New Testament people of God that describe Israel in the Old Testament. Thus, Jesus is the "living stone" (1 Pet 2:4), and so the New Testament people of God are

Paul also portrays the New Testament people of God in terms that consistently align with the Old Testament people of God. Thus, he declares that the Christ-followers in Philippi "are the true circumcision" (Phil 3:3). In the letter to the church in Colosse, Paul refers to the Christ-followers as "Those who have been chosen of God" (Col 3:12).[14]

The New Testament people of God fulfill the mission of God's people of being a light to the nations

The New Testament not only identifies the people of God with the Old Testament people of God, it also depicts them as carrying forth the mission to which Abraham and his descendants (Israel) were called. Thus, the followers of Christ, like Jesus himself, are the "light of the world" (Matt 5:14). Once again, the significance of this derives from the fact that being the light to the nations was the mission assigned to the Old Testament people of God (Isa 42:6; 49:6).

It is in accord with the New Testament people of God carrying forth the mission of Israel to be a light to the nations that Paul explicitly cites Isaiah 42:6 and 49:6 and applies them to himself and Barnabas,

> For thus the Lord has commanded us, "I have placed You as a light for the Gentiles, that you should bring salvation to the end of the earth" (Acts 13:47).

This citation carries significant weight in the present discussion. We have already observed that Simeon applied Isaiah 42:6 and 49:6 to Jesus (see Luke 2:32). There is no question that Jesus fulfills the role for the people of God as the light of the world.[15] The

---

"living stones" (1 Pet 2:5), and so is Israel (Isa 28:16). Thus, Jesus is "chosen" (1 Pet 2:4), and the New Testament people of God are "chosen" (1 Pet 2:9), and so is Israel (Isa 43:16–20).

14. As noted above, this accords with the fact that the Old Testament people of God are described as "My chosen people" (Isa 43:20).

15. Simeon had applied these Isaianic passages to Jesus in Luke 2:32.

question arises, however, as to how Paul could cite the very same passages and apply them to himself and Barnabas. The problem fades once we realize that although Jesus embodied the people of God by being a light to the nations, Jesus himself did not complete the mission. Jesus himself did not carry the mission of making God known to the nations. Instead, he commissions his followers to carry forth the mission to the nations:

> Go therefore and make disciples of all the nations (Matt 28:19).

The understanding that the New Testament people of God carry forth the mission of being a light to the nations corresponds with John's depiction of the people of God in the book of Revelation. In the opening vision in the book of Revelation, John sees Jesus walking in the midst of "seven lampstands" (Rev 1:12–13). Jesus affirms that the seven lampstands represent the seven churches (Rev 1:20). Using "lampstands" to depict the churches indicates their mission of being a light to the nations.

John's account of the two witnesses (Rev 11:1–13), which I believe is the central description of the people of God in the book of Revelation,[16] also depicts the people of God as faithfully performing the task of God's witnesses. In addition to being titled "My two witnesses" (Rev 11:3), they are also deemed, "The two lampstands" (Rev 11:4).[17]

Faith in Christ now identifies God's people

In the New Testament, faith in Christ becomes the primary means for identifying the people of God. Jesus explicitly declares,

> Behold My mother and My brothers! For whoever does the will of God, he is My brother and sister and mother (Mark 3:34–35).

---

16. See my *Revelation and the Two Witnesses*.

17. They are also depicted as carrying out the prophetic witness of Moses and Elijah (Rev 11:5–6).

In saying this, Jesus redefines the identity of the people of God around himself. From this point forward, the people of God are identified through faith in Jesus. Thus, Paul declares,

> For he is not a Jew who is one outwardly, neither is circumcision that which is outward in the flesh. But he is a Jew who is one inwardly; and circumcision is that which is of the heart, by the Spirit (Rom 2:28–29).

Consequently, Paul identifies Abraham as the father of "all who believe" (Rom 4:11). As a result, those who believe in Jesus are Abraham's descendants: "If you belong to Christ, then you are Abraham's offspring" (Gal 3:29).[18] In the same way, Peter declares that the faithful women within the community to which he wrote are descendants of Sarah,

> just as Sarah obeyed Abraham, calling him lord, and you have become her children if you do what is right without being frightened by any fear (1 Pet 3:6).

THE NEW JERUSALEM IS THE CONSUMMATION OF THE PEOPLE OF GOD

The new Jerusalem is a depiction of the people of God (the bride) dwelling in the presence of God in terms befitting a city/temple (Rev 21:9–22:9).[19] As such, it represents the consummation of God's desire that all the nations should dwell in his presence.[20]

---

18. Note that Galatians 3:29 follows Paul's affirmation in Galatians 3:28 that "There is neither Jew nor Greek . . ." Consequently, when he affirms that "you" are Abraham's offspring, he is referring to all of the people of God. The Greek corresponds with the Greek version of the promise to Abraham.

19. The new Jerusalem is introduced in Revelation 21:1–8 and then described in 21:9–22:9.

20. I am not suggesting that everyone is "saved" or that all go to the new Jerusalem. The account of the new Jerusalem in Revelation 21–22 indicates that this is not the case: "Outside are the dogs and the sorcerers and the immoral persons and the murderers and the idolaters, and everyone who loves and practices lying" (Rev 22:15).

The new Jerusalem is the embodiment of the people of God

The account of the new Jerusalem opens with John hearing an angel saying, "Come here, I shall show you the bride" (Rev 21:9). Instead of seeing the bride, however, John sees the holy city: he "showed me the holy city, Jerusalem, coming down out of heaven" (Rev 21:10). This raises the question as to whether John saw the bride or a city. The answer is that John saw the bride as a city/temple. Several features of the account of the new Jerusalem make this clear.

The identification of the bride with the new Jerusalem derives from John's opening description of the holy city, where John is told, "I will show you the bride" (Rev 21:9), but instead he is shown a city (Rev 21:10):

> Then one of the seven angels who had the seven bowls full of the seven last plagues came and spoke with me, saying, "Come here, I will show you the bride, the wife of the Lamb." And he carried me away in the Spirit to a great and high mountain, and showed me the holy city, Jerusalem, coming down out of heaven from God (Rev 21:9–10).

That John intends for us to identify the bride with the holy city stems from John's use of "hearing" and "seeing." Throughout the Apocalypse, John uses "hearing" and "seeing" to bring together two things that initially appear distinct. The most notable occurrence of "hearing" and "seeing" appears in Revelation 5:5–6. John first *hears* that the Lion has overcome (Rev 5:5). When he turns, however, doubtlessly to see the lion, he instead *sees* a "Lamb standing, as if slain" (Rev 5:6). We know, of course, that Jesus is both the Lion and the Lamb. Thus, in Revelation 21:9–22:9, John *hears* that he will see the bride, but instead, he *sees* the holy city. Consequently, the bride is the holy city, and the holy city is the bride.

In addition, the portrayal of the people of God as a city is evident from the contrast John establishes between the bride (Rev

21:9—22:9) and the great prostitute (Rev 17:1–19:10).[21] In the description of the great prostitute, John observes,

> The woman whom you saw is the great city, which reigns over the kings of the earth (17:18).

Just as the great prostitute is depicted as both as a city that is a woman, John similarly portrays the bride as a city that is a woman.[22]

The fact that the new Jerusalem represents the people of God is also evident in the description of the holy city, which abounds with features that correspond to the people of God. For example, the wall of the city contains twelve foundation stones, and "on them *were* the twelve names of the twelve apostles of the Lamb" (Rev 21:14). These foundation stones are adorned with twelve jewels (Rev 21:19–20), which themselves closely resemble the twelves jewels of the high priest's breastplate.[23] That the twelve jewels on the high priest's breastplate symbolized the twelve tribes of Israel, strongly implies that the holy city represents the people of God.

Finally, the fact that the holy city represents the people of God derives from John's repeated use of "twelve" to describe the city.[24] There is little question that twelve consistently refers to the people of God in both the Old Testament (twelve tribes) and the New Testament (twelve apostles). John not only uses twelve repeatedly in his description of the new Jerusalem, but there are twelve uses of twelve. John uses "twelve" three times in Revelation 21:12,[25]

---

21. The contrast between the Great Prostitute and Bride is apparent in the book of Revelation. For one, both are introduced in nearly identical ways (see Rev 17:1–3; 21:9–10). Also, both women are cities (17:18; 21:2, 9–10). See my commentary where I explore this issue in some detail: *Revelation: A Love Story*.

22. The holy city, new Jerusalem, is called the "new Jerusalem" in 21:2 and "Jerusalem" in 21:10.

23. See Exod 28:17–20; 39:8–14.

24. See my commentary for more details on John's use of numbers in the book of Revelation: *Revelation: A Love Story*.

25. There are "twelve" gates, "twelve" angels, and the names of the "twelve" tribes.

three times in 12:14,[26] once in 21:16,[27] two times in 21:21,[28] once in 22:2,[29] and there are two more in 21:17.[30] This surely indicates that the holy city is a portrait of the people of God dwelling in the presence of God.

The new Jerusalem as the combined Old Testament and New Testament people of God

The holy city, new Jerusalem, however, does not merely represent the people of God. It represents the combined people of God: i.e., the Old Testament and New Testament people of God together as one. This is evident from the fact that the city has the twelve gates with the names of the twelve tribes written on them (Rev 21:12), and it also has twelve foundation stones with the names of the twelve apostles on them (21:14). In addition, the walls of the city are 144 cubits (twelve times twelve) thick undoubtedly symbolizes the combined Old Testament and New Testament people of God.

The new Jerusalem as the dwelling place of all the nations

Although the new Jerusalem represents the combined presence of the Old Testament and New Testament saints, we cannot overlook

---

26. There are "twelve" foundation stones"; and "twelve" names of the "twelve" apostles.

27. The angel measures the city, and it is "12,000" stadia (Greek). Some English translations obscure the number in Greek by translating the size of the city in miles, but the ancients did not use miles.

28. The "twelve" gates are "twelve" pearls.

29. The Tree of Life has "twelve" fruits.

30. This one is more difficult to come by. John says that the city's wall is "144" cubits thick, which is 12 x 12 (Most English translations again obscure the Greek by translating the measurement into yards or feet, which the ancients did not use). The occurrences of two more twelves, therefore, is the result of 144 being the product of twelve times twelves. That John wants us to recognize the two uses of twelve embedded here is supported by the fact that the two uses of twelve here result in twelve uses of twelve.

the fact that the people of God in the new Jerusalem are composed of people from every nation. John affirms,

> The nations will walk by its light, and the kings of the earth will bring their glory into it. . . . And they will bring the glory and the honor of the nations into it (Rev 21:24, 26).

Moreover, the people from all the nations are uncountable:

> After these things I looked, and behold, a great multitude which no one could count, from every nation and *all* tribes and peoples and tongues, standing before the throne and before the Lamb (Rev 7:9).

By declaring that the nations who inhabit the new Jerusalem are uncountable, John confirms that the promise to Abraham regarding his descendants being as numerous as the stars of heaven is fulfilled in the book of Revelation by an uncountable multitude who are themselves from all the nations.

The significance of this cannot go unnoticed. Because the eschatological fulfillment of the promises of a family to Abraham occurs in the uncountable great multitude who hail from every nation, it is no wonder that the New Testament recognizes that the inclusion of the gentiles (the nations) into the one people of God constitutes the beginning of that fulfillment. Because the new Jerusalem signifies the place of God's presence among his people, we can now assert that the new Jerusalem represents the climactic[31] fulfillment of God's desire to dwell among all of humanity.

Are the Old Testament and New Testament people of God distinct for eternity?

At this point, some Christian Zionists contend that John's specifying that the gates of the new Jerusalem have the names of the twelve tribes written on them (Rev 12:12) and the foundation

---

31. One of the great works on the study of the book of Revelation is Richard Bauckham's aptly titled *The Climax of Prophecy*.

stones of the new Jerusalem have the names of the apostles written on them indicates that a distinction between the Old Testament people of God (Israel) and the New Testament people of God (the church) remains for all eternity.[32]

This suggestion, however, fails to understand that the names of the twelve tribes and the twelve apostles embedded in Revelation's holy city serve to affirm their unity and not their disunity. This unity is affirmed in that the walls are 144 cubits thick—the product of combining twelve and twelve. The twelve uses of twelve affirm the unity of the Old Testament and New Testament people of God in that there are not twenty-four uses of twelve. That the twelve foundation stones have the names of the twelve apostles on them (Rev 21:14) and that the twelve foundation stones are themselves adorned with twelve jewels, which correspond to the twelve jewels of the high priest's ephod—representing the twelve tribes—underscores the unity of the people of God.[33]

The notion that the Old Testament and New Testament people of God remain distinct for eternity also fails to account for the fact that the twelve apostles were all Jewish. How, then, can the twelve apostles be distinct from the Jewish people for eternity when they are themselves Jewish? And what about Jewish Christians and Messianic followers of Jesus today? Are they to be identified with the twelves tribes—seeing that they are ethnically Jewish—or with the twelve apostles—seeing that they affirm Christ?

Furthermore, the notion that the Jewish people remain distinct from the New Testament people of God throughout eternity betrays the fundamental message of the New Testament that there is only one people of God. As Paul says,

> For He Himself is our peace, who made both *groups into one* and broke down the barrier of the dividing wall, by abolishing in His flesh the enmity, *which is* the Law of commandments *contained* in ordinances, so that in

---

32. I have argued in detail that the 144,000 and the Great Multitude of Rev 7:1–17 are a unity. See my commentary, *Revelation: A Love Story*.

33. See Exod 28:17–20; 39:8–14.

Himself He might make the two into one new man, *thus* establishing peace (Eph 2:14–15).

Or, as Paul adds in Galatians,

> There is neither Jew nor Greek, there is neither slave nor free man, there is neither male nor female; for you are all one in Christ Jesus. And if you belong to Christ, then you are Abraham's descendants, heirs according to promise (Gal 3:28–29).[34]

Moreover, the classic and much debated Romans 9–11 affirms that the New Testament people of God are joined with the Old Testament people of God. Paul states,

> But if some of the branches were broken off, and you, being a wild olive, were grafted in among them and became partaker with them of the rich root of the olive tree (Rom 11:17)

Amidst all the interpretive difficulties in Romans 9–11, one thing is clear: the gentiles (the wild olive branches) are grafted into the tree that is Israel (the natural olive branches). The gentiles are not, in other words, grafted into a different tree, one that is distinct from Israel. Instead, some of the natural branches, which represent the Old Testament people of God that do not believe in Jesus, are cut off, and wild branches—representing the nations—are grafted in. There is only one tree. Moreover, that tree represents the people of God. That is, the physical descendants of Abraham are broken off, and believers from among the nations are grafted into a single tree.

---

34. Christian Zionists often respond that Galatians 3:28 is not absolute because "men remain men" and "women remain women." Therefore, they contend, "Jews remain Jews" and "gentiles remain gentiles." The problem is that this rejoinder misses Paul's point. Paul is not arguing that the rich are no longer rich and the poor are no longer poor. He argues that "in Christ," there are no distinctions. That is, the privileges that society might give to one who is male or rich over and against those who are female or poor are no longer recognized in Christ. Instead, the people of God are one—just as Adam and Eve were before they ate.

Also, the fact that the new Jerusalem represents the restoration of Eden, which I will elaborate on in chapter 6, affirms the continuity between the Old Testament and New Testament people of God. In Eden, Adam and Eve were one. They were, in fact, so unified in their identity that they did not recognize that nakedness (Gen 2:25).

Finally, Jesus' high priestly prayer affirms that the fulfillment aims to restore the unity of humanity:

> Holy Father, keep them in Your name, *the name* which You have given Me, that they may be one even as We *are* (John 17:11).

CONCLUSION

The people of God were called for a mission: to be a light to the nations. This mission was to be the means by which God would bless all nations. The New Testament affirms that Jesus, as the "seed" of Abraham, is the light of the world, and thus, he inaugurates the fulfillment of the mission. This mission is then carried forward through the Spirit by the New Testament people of God. The mission continues to be carried forth until it finds its ultimate fulfillment in the new Jerusalem, which is composed of people from all nations. Consequently, the New Testament affirms that the purpose of the people of God—to bless all the nations—has begun in Jesus, it continues—by means of the Spirit—in the life of the New Testament people of God today—who themselves are composed of people from many nations—and it climaxes in the New Jerusalem, where people from every nation enjoy the eternal presence of God among them.

The Christian Zionist's claim that the Old Testament people of God (Israel or the Jewish people) remain distinct from the New Testament people of God (the church) does not withstand scrutiny. Therefore, the Christian Zionist assertion that the covenant promises to Abraham and his descendants still apply to the physical descendants of Abraham fails to understand that Jesus and the

New Testament people of God are the descendants of Abraham, and through them that the very purpose for which God called Abraham and his descendants is fulfilled. The Christian Zionist claim that the covenant promises still apply to the Jewish people denies the fulfillment.

Whether or not the ethnic descendants of Abraham remain the chosen of God might be debated. However, even if we concede on this point, there is little doubt that they must come to faith in Christ to be reintegrated into the olive tree. The notion that they will be restored apart from Christ and the New Testament people of God betrays the New Testament. For,

> There is salvation in no one else; for there is no other name under heaven that has been given among men by which we must be saved (Acts 4:12).

6

THE BIBLICAL NARRATIVE AND THE LAND

I will give to you and to your descendants after you, the land of your sojournings, all the land of Canaan, for an everlasting possession; and I will be their God (Gen 17:8).

For the Lord has chosen Zion; He has desired it for His habitation. This is My resting place forever; Here I will dwell, for I have desired it (Ps 132:13–14).

Ask of Me, and I will surely give the nations as Your inheritance, And the very ends of the earth as Your possession (Psalm 2:8).

My thesis is that the Old Testament tabernacle and temples were symbolically designed to point to the cosmic eschatological reality that God's tabernacling presence, formerly limited to the holy of holies, was to be extended throughout the whole earth.[1]

---

1. Beale, *The Temple and the Church's Mission*, 25.

Part 2: A Biblical Theology of The Temple, The People, and The Land

SEVERAL YEARS AGO, *I co-taught a course on the prophets at a seminary in Nigeria. Before the first class began, I was making acquaintances with the students as they arrived. While talking with one of the students, I asked how far along he was in the program. He was excited to let me know that this was his last course. All he had left was his thesis. Naturally, I inquired as to what the topic of his thesis was.*

He replied, "I am writing on 'land' in the Old Testament."

I found that interesting, so I asked, "Have you considered writing on land in the New Testament?"

To my surprise, he said that though he had considered it, his advisor told him not to bother because "'Land' was not in the New Testament."

After a brief alarm, I replied, "Have you ever wondered why land is not in the New Testament?" I then asked a series of questions: "Is not land the most significant of the Old Testament promises? Do you not suspect that all of the rabbis at the time of Jesus were debating land? Do you not find it odd that the New Testament is silent on the land issue?"

After he replied "yes" to my queries, I encouraged him to think more deeply about why land is seemingly absent from the New Testament.

The following week, he approached me before class and admitted, "I cannot figure out why land is not in the New Testament." I suggested that we find a time to talk some more. That evening, we sat on the porch at the visiting faculty guest house and had a wonderful time searching the Scriptures to discern the nature of the land and the New Testament.

The promise of land[2] to Abraham and his descendants is reiterated throughout the book of Genesis (Gen 12:1, 7; 13:15; 15:18; 17:8; 24:7; 26:4; 28:13; 35:12) and much of the Old Testament (e.g., see: Exod 3:8; Deut 6:3; 1 Chr 16:18; 2 Chr 20:7; Ps 105:10–11). The land is unquestionably central to God's covenant promises.

---

2. The actual boundaries of the land promises are uncertain.

The Biblical Narrative and the Land

Christian Zionists appeal to the Old Testament's repetition of the land promise as key evidence for their assertion that the contemporary Jewish people retain a divine entitlement to the land.[3] That the land promise is occasionally stated as an "everlasting" promise (see Gen 17:8) reinforces the Christian Zionist conviction that the land not only belongs to the Jewish people but that it belongs to them in perpetuity. As one Christian Zionist writer contends,

> God has granted the title deed of the land of Israel to the Jewish people.... The land grant was both unconditional and eternal. Although the Jewish people might be disciplined with dispersion, their right to the land will never be removed.[4]

The fact that the land promise is conspicuous by its absence from the pages of the New Testament—or so it seems—lends further credence to the Christian Zionist contention that the promise of land to Abraham and his descendants still applies to the Jewish people.

I contend that, just as we saw concerning the promises of family to Abraham, the promise of land must also be understood through the lens of the temple and God's longing to abide among his people. The land promise to Abraham and his descendants was about establishing a sacred *place* where God's presence would reside and from which God would bless the entirety of the land.

---

3. Several years ago, a young man approached me at a conference, wanting to discuss the issue of land in the Scriptures. He was adamant that the Old Testament promises of land still applied to the Jewish people. When we met the next day, he proceeded to hand me thirty-five pages (this was before email and electronic communications) full of citations proving that the Old Testament promised the land to Abraham and his descendants. I explained to him that I agreed that the Old Testament is replete with promises of land to Abraham and his descendants. The question, however, is whether or not the promise of land is fulfilled in the pages of the New Testament.

I believe this is a common mistake in dialogues with Christian Zionists. They proceed from the Old Testament to the present day and skip over the New Testament. It is almost as if the New Testament is not permitted to have a voice on the issue.

4. Michael Rydelnik, *Understanding the Arab-Israeli Conflict*, 126, 157.

Part 2: A Biblical Theology of The Temple, The People, and The Land

THE ESCHATOLOGICAL FULFILLMENT OF THE LAND PROMISE

Christian Zionists often assert the everlastingness of the covenant promise of land in the Old Testament as evidence that the land promises still apply to the Jewish people. This assertion, however, entails two errors. First, it neglects the fact that Jesus is the consummate Israelite. If Jesus fulfills the promise, then the everlastingness is found in him. Second, it fails to account for the fact that for the present land to be God's "resting place forever" (Ps 132:14), an eschatological transformation becomes necessary. After all, the present city of Jerusalem "will pass away" (Rev 21:1) along with the present heavens and the earth.[5]

The author of Hebrews recognizes the eschatological nature of the land promise. The author of Hebrews observes that Abraham also recognized the eschatological nature of the land promise:

> For he [Abraham] was looking for the city which has foundations, whose architect and builder is God (Heb 11:10).

THE PURPOSE OF THE LAND PROMISE

Another element to consider when it comes to the fulfillment of the land promise relates to the purpose of the promise of land concerning the covenant. It is almost as though Christian Zionists believe that the purpose of the land promise was to provide a homeland for the Jewish people. The flaw in this conception lies in its failure to recognize the connection between the land promise and the Lord's desire to restore his Edenic presence to his creation.

Considering this, I will argue that God intended for the land to serve as the *place* where he would dwell among his people. In addition, the land would also function as the center from which the knowledge of God would spread to the nations. As the knowledge of God spreads, God's presence, which would come to indwell his

---

5. See also 1 John 2:17.

people, would expand as well. Ultimately, at the consummation, the result will be, "The whole earth is full of His glory" (Isa 6:3).

TEMPORARY PROVISIONS UNTIL THE FULFILLMENT

Another crucial aspect to consider regarding the land is that in the same way, the tabernacle of Moses and the temple building limited the presence of God to one locale, the allocation of one particular land also restricted God's presence to that one place. Consequently, as long as the land remained confined to one geographical location, it would be unable to fulfill God's desire to dwell among all humanity and throughout the entirety of the creation.

JESUS AS THE LAND

Once again, the fulfillment of the land promise is revealed in Jesus. Given that Jesus embodies the temple presence of God, it naturally follows that he embodies the land as well.

That Jesus embodies the land is apparent in the New Testament, where fundamental symbols associated with the land are consistently attributed to him. For example, one of the primary symbols in the Old Testament for the land was the vineyard (See Ps 80:8–19; Isa 5:1–7; 27:2–6; Jer 2:21; 5:10; 12:11–13; Ezek 15:1–8; 17:1–10; 19:10–14). In light of this, Jesus unmistakably identifies himself with the land when he declares, "I am the vine, you are the branches" (John 15:5). Similarly, Jesus ascribes attributes of the land to himself when he asserts that he is the "bread of life" (John 6:35, 48, 51).

The significance of Jesus as the fulfillment of the land promise lies in the New Testament affirmation that our sustenance no longer depends on the land for bread but on Jesus himself. Jesus, not the land, is now the source of our sustenance for the people of God (i.e., he is the bread of life).

Part 2: A Biblical Theology of The Temple, The People, and The Land

THROUGH THE SPIRIT THE NEW TESTAMENT PEOPLE OF GOD ARE THE FULFILLMENT OF THE LAND

In the New Testament, the Spirit fills the people of God, and they become the place of God's temple presence. They then take the gospel to the nations, and the promised land expands with them.[6]

The affirmation that the New Testament people of God currently embody the dwelling place of God (i.e., the temple) is evident throughout the New Testament.[7] In 1 Corinthians 6:19, Paul declares,

> Or do you not know that your body is a temple of the Holy Spirit who is in you.

If the temple represents the place of God's presence, and if, by means of the indwelling of the Spirit, the followers of Christ are themselves God's temple, then the place of God's presence has expanded from Christ himself to the New Testament people of God.

That the people of God have become the place of God's temple presence and that this corresponds to the land promise is evident in Paul's declaration in 2 Corinthians 6:16:

> For we are the temple of the living God.

In making this assertion, it is critical to note that Paul justifies his claim that the Corinthians are the temple of God by citing the covenant promise of Leviticus 26:12 and Ezekiel 37:27:

> just as God said, "I will dwell in them and walk among them; And I will be their God, and they shall be My people" (2 Cor 6:16).

This is critical. Paul cites the covenant affirmation of God's desire to dwell among his people, found in Leviticus and reiterated in

---

6. I suppose that some might struggle to see how an inanimate entity such as "land" can be fulfilled in a person. The answer to this is simple: Jesus is the temple. Jesus is the bread of life. Many inanimate things point to Christ as the fulfillment.

7. See also 1 Cor 3:16–17; 2 Cor 6:14–18; Eph 2:18–22.

Ezekiel. He claims that the Spirit's indwelling of the Christ-followers in Corinth constitutes the fulfillment of the covenant promises. Consequently, the Christ-followers in Corinth are now the place of God's presence in accord with the Old Testament covenant promise of land.

The New Testament people of God are presently heirs of the land

Another critical element that illustrates the present fulfillment of the land promise in the New Testament is the frequent application of inheritance language to the New Testament people of God. For example, Paul affirms,

> Whatever you do, do your work heartily, as for the Lord rather than for men, knowing that from the Lord you will receive the reward of the inheritance (Col 3:23-24).

Peter likewise declares,

> Blessed be the God and Father of our Lord Jesus Christ, who according to His great mercy has caused us to be born again to a living hope through the resurrection of Jesus Christ from the dead, to *obtain* an inheritance *which is* imperishable and undefiled and will not fade away, reserved in heaven for you . . . (1 Pet 1:3-4).

This raises the question, "What are the New Testament people of God heirs of?" At this point, the Christian Zionist might assert that the inheritance pertains to "salvation."[8] It is critical, however, to recognize the biblical correlation between the inheritance and the promises concerning family and land.[9] The correspondence

---

8. Unpacking this significance transcends the limited scope of this present work. Suffice it to say that in the Old Testament, the promise of family and land are intertwined with what we might want to call "eternal life." This is evident in Psalm 37. Furthermore, the common attribution of such verses to our "salvation" betrays an Epicurean worldview.

9. This does not intend to deny that "salvation" is not also a part of our inheritance.

between the promise of inheritance in the New Testament and the land is evident in Jesus' affirmation,

> "Blessed are the gentle, for they shall inherit the earth" (Matt 5:5).

Moreover, there is the natural assumption that if we, through faith in Jesus, have become the children of Abraham, then the promises made to our forefather Abraham also apply to us. This is what Paul affirms when he says,

> And if you belong to Christ, then you are Abraham's descendants, heirs according to promise (Gal 3:29).

To argue that the New Testament promise of inheritance excludes the land contravenes the straightforward reading of the text. After all, being a descendant of Abraham included the right to inherit the land. To propose that the New Testament people of God do not inherit the land would imply that we are not indeed the children of Abraham. Furthermore, the abundant references throughout the Old Testament that the people will inherit the land virtually demands that the inheritance in the New Testament refers to the land.[10]

Land becomes the whole Earth

The land promise expands in the New Testament and continues to expand until the descent of the new Jerusalem. At that time, the "whole earth will be full of His glory" (Isa 6:3).

Expanding the place of God's presence also corresponds with the missional call of God's people. In the New Testament, the people of God are no longer restricted to one nation and one place, and because they go into all of the earth, the place of God's presence is no longer limited to one land. Jesus explicitly declares that

---

10. Ironically, Christian Zionists often contend that non-Zionist Christians "spiritualize" the promises when, in fact, it is they who are spiritualizing. After all, the Christian Zionist contends that the inheritance for the New Testament people of God is "salvation" and not the land.

the inheritance of land is no longer tied to the land of Israel but that it now extends to the whole earth when he declares: "Blessed are the gentle, for they shall inherit the earth" (Matt 5:5).

Paul's understanding that the land promise now applies to the entire earth is evident in his exhortation for children to obey their parents: "Children, obey your parents in the Lord, for this is right" (Eph 6:1). Paul references the Old Testament command, as found in Deuteronomy 5:16, and notes that it contains a promise: "HONOR YOUR FATHER AND MOTHER (which is the first commandment with a promise), SO THAT IT MAY BE WELL WITH YOU, AND THAT YOU MAY LIVE LONG ON THE EARTH" (Eph 6:2–3). Interestingly, in Ephesians 6:3, Paul uses the Greek word "*ge*" ("land" or "earth"). This word is traditionally applied to the promised land. What is important to note is that Paul is writing to Christ's followers in Ephesus (i.e., those not in the land of Israel). This suggests that Ephesians 6:3 must be understood as the "earth."[11] After all, Paul's affirmation that the Ephesian children who honor their parents will live long in the "land" of Israel would hardly have much of an appeal. If, however, the promise was that they would live long on the "earth," then Paul's application of it for the Christ-followers in Ephesus makes sense.

Paul also declares that the promise of land to Abraham and his descendants now extends to the world in his letter to Rome: "For the promise to Abraham or to his descendants that he would be heir of the world . . ." (Rom 4:13). In this instance, Paul substitutes "world" (Gk *kosmos*) for "land" (Gk *ge*). Therefore, while one might argue that in Ephesians 6:3 the promise applied specifically to the land and not the entirety of the earth, Paul's affirmation in Romans 4:13 eliminates any room for such ambiguity. The land promise expands to include the entire world.

---

11. All major English translations use "earth" here except the ESV, which employs "land."

Part 2: A Biblical Theology of The Temple, The People, and The Land

THE NEW JERUSALEM AS THE ESCHATOLOGICAL FULFILLMENT OF THE LAND PROMISES

The most definitive fulfillment of the New Testament's land promise is found in the new Jerusalem. As I noted at the beginning of this chapter, the Christian Zionist contention that the land promise applies exclusively to the present physical land and to the physical descendants of Abraham because it is an "everlasting" covenant encounters an insurmountable problem: The present city of Jerusalem will not last forever. Therefore, the consummation of the land promises must refer to the new Jerusalem.

That the new Jerusalem represents the eschatological fulfillment of the land promises derives from the fact that it represents the eternal dwelling place of God among his people. As noted in our discussion of the temple in chapter 4, Rev 21:1-8 introduces the new Jerusalem with language connecting it with the covenant promises of Leviticus 26:12-13 and Ezekiel 37:26-27:

> Behold, the tabernacle of God is among men, and He will dwell among them, and they shall be His people, and God Himself will be among them.... He who overcomes will inherit these things, and I will be his God, and he will be My son (Rev 21:3, 7).

The fact that the new Jerusalem embodies the fulfillment of God's eternal dwelling place among his people reinforces the conviction that it represents the fulfillment of God's desire to dwell among his people.

The account of the new Jerusalem explicitly affirms that it represents the eternal dwelling place of God among his people. John states,

> The Lord God the Almighty and the Lamb are its temple (Rev 21:22).

That God's throne is in the new Jerusalem also affirms that it is a temple.

> The throne of God and of the Lamb will be in it (Rev 22:3)

Even more emphatically, John declares that in the new Jerusalem, all the people of God

> will see His face (Rev 22:4).[12]

New Jerusalem as the restored Eden

Another essential feature of the new Jerusalem is that John's portrait of the new Jerusalem corresponds with Eden.

The relationship between the new Jerusalem and Eden appears in John's description of "a river of the water of life, clear as crystal, coming from the throne of God and of the lamb" (22:1). This river of the water of life corresponds with the river in Eden: "Now a river flowed out of Eden to water the garden" (Gen 2:10). Even more evident is the presence in the new Jerusalem of the "tree of life" (Rev 22:2), which most certainly alludes to the tree of life in Genesis 2:9.[13] Finally, that the new Jerusalem represents the restoration of Eden is evident in that in the new Jerusalem, "there will no longer be any curse" (22:3), which surely indicates the reversing of the curse upon the land in Genesis 3:17.

---

12. See Heb 9:7. The holy of holies represents the place where God dwelt, and it is the place where the high priest was permitted to enter the presence of God once per year. If John's description of the holy city is meant to be understood in terms of the holy of holies, then it is no surprise to learn that all those who enter the city will experience the glorious presence of God and "will see His face" (22:4).

13. Although a discussion of John's account of the new Jerusalem and Ezekiel's eschatological temple (see Ezek 40–48) will take us too far afield, it behooves us to note that John's description of the river of life and the tree of life as well as the fact that the leaves of the tree of life in the new Jerusalem are "for the healing of the nations" (Rev 22:2) most certainly corresponds to Ezekiel's temple (see Ezek 47:1–12). Interestingly, the leaves of the tree in Ezekiel are "for healing" (Ezek 47:12), whereas, for John, they are "for the healing of the nations" (Rev 22:2). Once again, we see another example of the fulfillment expanding: in this instance so that it includes the nations.

The new Jerusalem fills the earth

Finally, there is good reason to believe that the new Jerusalem fills the entirety of the earth. In his description of the new Jerusalem, John notes that an angel measures the city. Its dimensions are "12,000 stadia"[14] (roughly 1,400–1,500 miles) in every direction (Rev 21:16). Interestingly, the dimensions of the city extend well beyond that of Jerusalem and the promised land. This corresponds with my argument that just as the promise of family to Abraham expands—as it now includes those who have faith in Jesus, the land promise also expands.

The size of the city, however, does not simply suggest that it extends beyond the boundaries of the ancient promised land but fills the whole of the new creation. That the new Jerusalem expands so that it fills the entirety of the new creation is suggested by the fact that twelve thousand stadia correspond roughly to the dimensions of the Roman empire, which, for those in the Roman empire, extended to the "whole world."[15]

New Jerusalem as the holy of holies

Finally, John's description of the new Jerusalem is linked solely with the holy of holies within the temple. That is, the entirety of the new Jerusalem corresponds to the inner sanctum of the temple. The significance of this is that the holy of holies is the specific location of God's throne.

That the holy of holies comprises the entirety of the new Jerusalem and gains support from the fact that the measurements of the holy city correspond to the holy of holies and not the entirety of the temple building. John says that the holy city was measured

---

14. My translation. Since numbers play a significant role in the book of Revelation, it is likely that the significance of "12,000 stadia" lies in the use of twelve.

15. John would indeed have been aware that Rome did not inhabit the entire earth. The New Testament writers did, however, employ "the whole world" even though they meant only the Roman world: see Romans 1:8.

(Rev 21:15–17) and "the city is laid out as a square" (Rev 21:16). The city, however, is not just a square but a cube. John adds, "Its length and width and height are equal" (21:16). This corresponds to the dimensions of the holy of holies: "The inner sanctuary was twenty cubits in length, twenty cubits in width, and twenty cubits in height" (1 Kgs 6:20).

CONCLUSION

As I intimated at the beginning of this chapter, the promise of land appears to be missing from the pages of the New Testament. This apparent absence is not due to its actual absence but to the nature of the fulfillment. As long as we assume that the land promise applies only to the physical descendants of Abraham occupying a specific piece of land, it indeed appears that the New Testament is silent concerning the land. I hope to have shown in this chapter that land promise underlies the entirety of the New Testament. The promise of land finds its fulfillment first in Jesus, then with the New Testament people of God, and finally in the new Jerusalem. This becomes evident once we recognize that the land promise was intimately connected with the temple. The land was to be the place in which the temple was located.

The promise of land, therefore, points us to Christ because he is the temple presence of God and, as such, he is the source of sustenance for the New Testament people of God. Then, through the indwelling of the Spirit, the people of God are commissioned to go to the nations. As they do so, the presence of God extends with them. The promise of land then climaxes in the new Jerusalem, which represents God's presence among his people. That the new Jerusalem encompasses the entirety of the new creation means that, indeed,

> The whole earth is full of His glory (Isa 6:3).

7

IS THIS REPLACEMENT THEOLOGY?

THROUGHOUT THE CHURCH'S HISTORY, numerous individuals have subscribed to various iterations of replacement theology. Contemporary proponents, however, are exceedingly rare. Nonetheless, the allegation of replacement theology has not diminished. Unfortunately, the charge of replacement theology has been weaponized. It is often used to suppress dissenting voices.

WHAT IS REPLACEMENT THEOLOGY?

Replacement theology posits that since the ethnic descendants of Abraham (Jewish people) disobeyed the covenant with God, God has rejected them and chose to *replace* them with those who believe in Jesus. In other words, replacement theology posits that "Israel" has been *replaced* by "the church." Because adherents of replacement theology have historically been proponents of antisemitism, and their antisemitism has often been accompanied by violence against the Jewish community, it goes without saying that replacement theology is problematic.

Is This Replacement Theology?

WHY I AM NOT A REPLACEMENT THEOLOGIAN[1]

What I have argued is not replacement theology. The reason for this is that in my view neither Jesus nor those who believe in him replace ethnic Israel. Jesus does not replace Israel because he is Israel. Christians do not replace Israel either. Instead, as I argued in chapter 5, those who believe in Jesus are grafted into the olive tree that is Israel:

> You, being a wild olive, were grafted in among them and became partaker with them of the rich root of the olive tree (Rom 11:17).

This means that there are not two trees (one being Israel and the other being the church). As Paul says, Abraham is "the father of all who believe" (Rom 4:11).

Replacement theology, which is often considered to be synonymous with supersessionism, claims that the church "replaces" Israel. The problem with this understanding is that it often betrays a "literal" versus a "spiritual" binary. The argument assumes that in the Old Testament, God's promises were "literal" promises made to the ethnic descendants of Abraham. Whereas, in the New Testament, it is assumed the promises are "spiritual" and applied to those who believe in Jesus. This binary thinking is problematic because it fails to understand the larger narrative and the missional call for Abraham and his descendants. I have argued in this work that Jesus, and through the Spirit, the New Testament people of God fulfill the missional call for Abraham and his descendants.

---

1. I have written about this extensively in my book *These Brothers of Mine*, 98–103.

8

CONCLUSION

In early 2012, I was part of a delegation that attended a midmorning briefing by the National Security Council (NSC) at the White House Conference Center. Our group comprised Israelis, Palestinians, Americans, human rights workers, and various Jewish, Muslim, and Christian leaders. It was the final year of Obama's first term in office. Before the meeting, many of us were dismayed by the fact that President Obama, who had expressed a deep desire to find a solution to the Israeli-Palestinian conflict, had made little to no progress on the issue. We were hoping for an explanation. We soon discovered that he was not about to make progress anytime soon.

For the first thirty-five minutes of our time together, the NSC spokesperson made it clear that the Obama administration was not going to engage this issue in a timely fashion. After all, it was an election year. The spokesperson reiterated the same point in various ways: "The US government does not negotiate with terrorists."

In the hours after Hamas's incursion into Israel on October 7, President Biden employed the same line in his speech affirming the United States' support for Israel. For Biden, this refrain served as a justification for war. He affirmed Israel's right to respond with violence and that the US had Israel's back; he even added, "Full stop." In the case of our briefing with the NSC, "We don't negotiate with

Conclusion

terrorists" meant, "We are not going to act because it is not politically expedient for us to do so during an election year."

Of course, the "We don't negotiate with terrorists" line is simply nonsense. There is always a workaround. In the days after the Hamas attack of October 7, the US and the Israelis negotiated with Hamas through a third party—the government of Qatar. That is how they negotiated a cease-fire, which included a hostage exchange, in November of 2023.

During the NSC briefing, the longer the spokesperson talked, the more and more disillusioned I became at our elected officials and their unwillingness to do what is right (in this instance, what was best for Israelis, Palestinians, and the US), simply because it is not politically advantageous for them. I soon learned I wasn't the only disillusioned person in the room.

After thirty-five minutes of saying the same thing, the spokesperson opened the floor for questions. The first question came from a wonderful Jewish-Israeli woman who had been working towards a just peace in the land for some time. She rose and, though small in stature, responded, "What do you mean the US doesn't negotiate with terrorists?" Then, without enough time to even catch a breath, she exclaimed, "The US negotiated with the IRA and with . . ." (she rattled off four more examples so quickly I could hardly keep up with her). Her point: the US negotiates with terrorists all the time. When she finished, the NSC spokesperson incredibly replied, "The US doesn't negotiate with terrorists." Yep. He reiterated the one point he had made for the past thirty-five minutes. It was obvious that nothing could be said to change the official US position during an election year.

To leave the conference center, we had to proceed in two parallel lines through the security scanner through which we had entered. As I exited, bishop Ronnie Crudup stood beside me. I looked at Bishop Crudup and asked him: "Bishop, what do you do with that?" He looked back at me smiling, as only Bishop Crudup can, and said, "Rob, if you want to see any real change, it is up for us to do it."

Part 2: A Biblical Theology of The Temple, The People, and The Land

THE MISSION OF GOD'S PEOPLE

Unfortunately, many Christians have an overly simplistic conception of their Christian calling that conceives of our task in terms of a form of personal spirituality; we must grow in sanctification and perhaps tell others about Jesus when we can.

This Christian mission, however, entails making Christ known to the nations.[1] This is significant because God makes himself known to the world through us. Moreover, as I noted previously, we make Christ known by reflecting who he is. Jesus affirmed, "By this all men will know that you are My disciples, if you have love for one another" (John 13:35). In other words, it is through loving others that we reflect who God is.

But Jesus' kind of love is a cross-bearing, sacrificial love for the sake of the other. When we sacrificially surrender ourselves for the sake of others (which is the hallmark of Christian love), we tell the world, "This is what our God looks like." When we demonstrate a radical, cross-bearing, sacrificial love for the other, we proclaim Jesus. The same Jesus who died for you and me died for the world. And he demonstrated that love on the cross. This is what the famed John 3:16 means when it says, "For God so loved the world . . ." It is this sort of love for our enemies that Jesus calls all Christians to in the Sermon on the Mount:

> But I say to you, love your enemies and pray for those who persecute you, so that you may be sons of your Father who is in heaven; for He causes His sun to rise on *the* evil and *the* good, and sends rain on *the* righteous and *the* unrighteous (Matt 5:44–45).

The implication is clear: when we love our enemies, we act like children of the Father. Why is that? Because God loves his enemies, he "causes His sun to rise on *the* evil and *the* good, and sends rain on *the* righteous and *the* unrighteous" (Matt 5:45).

When it comes to the people of Israel, Gaza, the West Bank, or Iran, many Christians are decidedly in favor of Israel. There is a

---

1. I do not deny that this begins with us individually and corporately growing in the likeness and image of Christ (Col 1:28–29).

Conclusion

sense in which this is fine. After all, Christians' support for Israelis is an example of loving our neighbor. The question arises, however, "Why is the same Christian charity not extended to Palestinians, Iranians, and the people of every other nation?"[2] Are we not called to love even our enemies? Are we not to weep with them when they suffer loss? Are we not to plead with our nation to not kill them, just as we plead with them not to kill Israelis?

I fear that Christians' "love for Israel" has become dangerous. It is dangerous for Israelis and Palestinians, Americans, Iranians, and the people of almost every other nation. But more than this, it is dangerous to Christ and the kingdom.

---

2. At determinetruth.com, we recently did a livestream with an Iranian Christian pastor who told us how wonderful and kind the people of Iran are and how much they love Americans. We must understand that the people of these countries, every country, are just like us: they are moms and dads, and sons and daughters; they want to live in peace and raise a family with the hope that they will have a future. Demonizing the other is what nations do because it makes it easier to justify going to war against them. (See https://www.youtube.com/watch?v=ZYJs96S2TCs.)

PART 3

APPLICATION AND JUSTICE

9

LOOKING AT THE ISRAELI-PALESTINIAN CONFLICT THROUGH THE LENS OF THE KINGDOM OF GOD

I FIND IT INCREDIBLE that, although God called the church to make him known by manifesting his love to our enemies, we are more often known for advocating for war and justifying violence against them. Encouraging war is neither Christian nor loving. Tragically, while much of the world calls for a cease-fire and a just solution to the war on Gaza, it is mainly Western Christians who continue to encourage war and the destruction of Gaza. The church needs to understand that non-Christians have a pretty low view of us—and that is being generous. Do we not see the irony here? Can we not see that we are advocating for the things that contradict the gospel and the kingdom? Are not Christians to be on the side that advocates for a just peace instead of the side of war and violence?

In acknowledging this, I understand nations cannot adopt a kingdom of God ethic. One world leader cannot say to another, "Go ahead and slap me on the right cheek. I'll love you anyway." This reality, however, underscores the church's vital role in speaking truth to power. A just peace is the only solution to bring an end to violence. After all,

> All those who take up the sword shall perish by the sword (Matt 26:52).

At the same time, I concede that a just peace may not always work. My point, however, is that the church must never concede to violence as if it is the best or the only solution. This is what Jesus meant when he said, "Those who take up the sword shall perish by the sword" (Matt 26:52). Violence leads to more violence. Consequently, even if we agreed that Israel has a right to defend itself, it behooves us to warn them that a violent response will almost certainly make matters worse.

This means that to love Israelis and Palestinians, we must advocate for a just and peaceful solution to this conflict. And we must do so now. This conviction is true regardless of our theological convictions as to whether or not the Jewish people are God's chosen people and whether or not the promise of land still applies to them.

10

IS IT OKAY TO CRITIQUE ISRAEL? ISRAEL AND ANTISEMITISM

IS IT OKAY TO CRITIQUE ISRAEL?

WHEN IT COMES TO the Israeli-Palestinian conflict, it is my concern that Western Christians have abdicated our responsibility to pursue peace and justice.

There is no question that some of the blame for the current tensions resides with the Palestinian leadership, who have not done enough to care for the Palestinian people. Palestinians have resorted to violence. Suicide bombings and terrorist attacks, like that of October 7, have marred this conflict. But much blame also resides with the Israeli leadership. The Israeli government has continued to expand the settlement enterprise,[1] which results in the

---

1. "Settlements" are illegal (they are illegal by Israeli law and by international law) outposts or cities established inside the West Bank (i.e., Palestinian territory). To date, more than 700,000 Israeli settlers are living in over two hundred settlements in the West Bank. The problematic nature of these settlements is hard to overstate. For one, the land upon which these settlements are built is land that belongs to the Palestinians and is vital if there is ever to be a future Palestinian state. That so much of the West Bank has been stolen by the Israeli settlements virtually precludes the possibility of a future Palestinian state. Second, much of the violence in the West Bank is perpetrated by the ideological settlers. Such violence against Palestinians in the West Bank has increased significantly since the attack of October 7.

loss of land for Palestinians—land that is vital to an independent state for the Palestinians. The Israeli Defense Forces have imposed oppressive restrictions on the Palestinians in the occupied territories, including restricting movement and limiting access to water and other necessities. They have continued to "detain" Palestinians—including thousands of children between the ages of twelve and seventeen—holding them in oppressive conditions in Israeli military prisons.[2] Concerning the Gaza Strip, Israel imposed a complete air, land, and sea blockade. As a result, the UN had declared that by 2020, Gaza would be unlivable.

I suspect that many readers may experience a measure of hesitation or even resistance at this point. The word "but" wants to come out: "But" doesn't Israel have a right to self-defense? "But" how can Israel make peace with an enemy that wants to eradicate them? "But" Israel pulled out of Gaza in 2005, and look at what happened. "But" we are loving the Jewish people by advocating for the destruction of their enemies. We love the people of Gaza also, "but" Israel has no choice but to eradicate Hamas. We love the people of Gaza, "but" it is their fault because they elected Hamas. But, but, but.

I am not suggesting that these "but" statements are untrue. My concern is that when we affirm Israel's right to self-defense even when their actions exceed the legitimacy of what can be deemed self-defense and thereby justify, or look past, the deaths of tens of thousands in Gaza, and the injustices committed against Palestinians in the West Bank. My concern is when we approach the Israeli-Palestinian conflict as if Israel has done nothing wrong.

I have had many conversations with leading Christian Zionists who regularly acknowledge that Israel is not perfect and that Israel, like every other nation, makes mistakes. Yet, when pressed for specific examples of Israel's mistakes, they consistently fail to provide any. Even when the entire international community agrees

---

2. The number of "detainees" in Israeli prisons has increased dramatically since October 7. Yet, this was one of the primary reasons that Hamas stated for its attack. If Israel and the Palestinians are going to work towards peace, then Israel's detaining of Palestinians needs to diminish if not disappear.

that Israel is on a path to genocide, many Christian Zionists offer little to no condemnation.

WHY ARE THERE SPECIAL RULES OF ENGAGEMENT WHEN DISCUSSING ISRAEL?

Another difficulty with dialogues related to Israel's assault on Gaza and its continued occupation in the West Bank is that questioning Israel's actions is only permitted if we first agree to specific stipulations. For instance, before we can question the legitimacy of Israel's assault on Gaza—which the International Court of Justice considers plausibly to involve Israel in committing genocide—we cannot proceed unless we first unequivocally condemn Hamas's acts of terror on October 7, 2023.[3] Can it not be true that Hamas's acts of terror on October 7 were damnable but so also has been Israel's response? Or, that before addressing Israel's oppressive occupation of the Palestinian territories and its continuous expansion of the settlement enterprise, it must first be met with acknowledgment of Israel's existential fear of annihilation. It is as if Israel's oppression of the Palestinians is justified—regardless of how oppressive it is—because they have a legitimate existential fear of annihilation. Once again, we must ask, "Can it not be true that Israel has a legitimate existential fear, yet they are carrying out injustices in their occupation of the West Bank and their continuous settlement expansion?"

ANTISEMITISM

Antisemitism is alive and well in the world today. Unfortunately, Christians have been some of the most ardent antisemites in history. As a community called to love our enemies (Matt 5:44) and

---

3. I have no problem in condemning Hamas's actions of October 7. Violence against civilians is unacceptable. But why must this be the starting point for the conversation? Why can we not begin with Israel's oppressive blockade of the Gaza Strip that forced 2.3 million people to live in an open-air prison (which some labeled an open-air concentration camp)?

to advocate for the oppressed (Isa 1:17; Ps 82:3–4), we must denounce antisemitism and stand against injustices directed at the Jewish people.

At the same time, it is critical to distinguish between antisemitism and legitimate criticism of a secular state. In the same way that critiquing the United States is not inherently anti-American (in fact, exercising one's right to free speech and using it to condemn the US when it acts unjustly might very well be one of the most patriotic acts), so also criticizing the state of Israel does not necessarily entail antisemitism. This acknowledgment does not deny that criticizing Israel can encourage and even lead to antisemitism or that such criticisms may contain antisemitic tropes.

Leveling the charge of antisemitism against valid criticisms of the state of Israel often renders the state of Israel immune from criticism. Enabling any state actors to act with impunity is dangerous. After all, every state is subject to rogue politicians. This becomes even more dangerous when politicians cannot be held in check by valid criticism.

In addition, when accusations of antisemitism are too hastily applied, they undermine the gravity of genuine acts of antisemitism. Real antisemitism has resulted in murderous atrocities such as the 2018 shooting at the Tree of Life Synagogue in Pittsburgh and a host of other violent crimes, not to mention the pogroms of Europe and the Nazi Holocaust. We should not diminish the evils of antisemitism and the dangers it brings by coupling honest attempts to critique a secular government with hatred and acts of violence directed at the Jewish people.

CONFLATING "ISRAEL" WITH "ISRAEL"

One of the dangerous elements of Christian Zionism is that the Western Church's Israel-centrism dangerously conflates "Israel" (the Jewish people) with "Israel" (the modern nation-state).

The modern state of Israel is a secular state. Twenty percent of its citizens are not even Jewish, they are Arab citizens of Israel. Furthermore, the state of Israel is a nation, and like every other

Is It Okay to Critique Israel? Israel and Antisemitism

nation, it is not perfect. Supporting Israel as a state today often means endorsing the policies of Israeli Prime Minister Benjamin Netanyahu and the far-right extremists that are a part of his coalition government.

Unfortunately, because we have conflated "Israel" with "Israel," it has become unacceptable to criticize the state of Israel. Inside the evangelical church, criticizing Israel is often viewed as a sort of abandonment of our God-given responsibility to "bless" Israel. But criticizing someone when they do wrong is what it means to love them. Allowing someone to continue in their destructive behavior is not loving. Loving Israel to the point that we ignore the nation's destructive actions is selfish. It reflects a mindset more concerned with one's actions (blessing Israel) than with the object of our "love." This is not love. I fear that Israel's behavior over the last several months, not to speak of the past few decades (they have been building settlements in the West Bank for over fifty-five years and oppressively occupying the West Bank and Gaza since 1967), may well lead to the destruction of Israel. Allowing this to happen is not loving to Israelis, let alone the Palestinians.

The inability to criticize and condemn Israel has repeatedly been demonstrated since the acts of October 7. Time and time again, Christians aim to justify Israel's acts of injustice. When Israel bombs a hospital and kills everyone inside, it is justified because Hamas was using it as a base of operations. When Israel shuts off food, water, and gas to the 2.3 million people, it is justified because such necessities would allow Hamas to strengthen. When Israel bombs a refugee camp, it is justified because a key Hamas leader was present. When Israel bombs the Iranian consulate in Syria (which is considered Iranian territory), we stay silent. But when Iran retaliates, we are outraged.

Can we genuinely consider the seventeen thousand new orphans in Gaza as justifiable because Israel has a right to self-defense? Can we account for the demolition of Gaza's largest hospital (al Shifa) and the killing of everyone inside, not to mention rendering twenty-four of the other thirty-five hospitals in Gaza inoperable, because Hamas uses hospitals as human shields? Can we defend the displacement of 1.9 million people (some of them having been displaced multiple times previously) because Israel must eliminate Hamas, and Israel warned them by sending millions of leaflets? What about older people, people with disabilities, and others who are unable to leave? Are they merely collateral damage? Can we look past the thousands of children who have had amputations without anesthesia because Israel must limit supplies into Gaza to ensure that Hamas cannot regather? What about the large segments of the population in Gaza that are on the brink of famine because Israel limits supplies?

CONCLUSION

My concern is that we have become unable to see some of the injustices because of our "love" for the Jewish people. But in our effort to love Israel, have we betrayed the gospel? In our effort to love Israel, have we become unwilling and, at times, even unable to criticize the nation of Israel? Because we are unable to see injustices as injustices, I believe that we have failed to recognize that the present war on Gaza and the ongoing occupation of the West Bank—including the continued confiscation of Palestinians' lands and the expansion of settlements—is not good for Israel or the Jewish people. To love the Jewish people—whether it be because one believes they remain the chosen people of God or because Christ commands us to love everyone—requires us to demand that the state of Israel do what is just.

11

THE MIRACLE OF 1948?

The best explanation is that the modern state of Israel seems to be a dramatic work of God in fulfillment of the Bible's predictions of a Jewish return to the land of Israel.[1]

For I will take you from the nations, gather you from all the lands and bring you into your own land. Then I will sprinkle clean water on you, and you will be clean; I will cleanse you from all your filthiness and from all your idols. Moreover, I will give you a new heart and put a new spirit within you; and I will remove the heart of stone from your flesh and give you a heart of flesh. I will put My Spirit within you and cause you to walk in My statutes, and you will be careful to observe My ordinances. You will live in the land that I gave to your forefathers; so you will be My people, and I will be your God (Ezek 36:24–28).

As a young follower of Christ, I adhered to Christian Zionism. My convictions derived from my belief that the rebirth of the state of Israel in 1948 was a miracle brought about by God. Not only did I believe that God miraculously restored Israel to the land, but the

---

1. Rydelnik, *Understanding the Arab-Israeli Conflict*, 132.

formation of the state of Israel provided support for my beliefs about biblical prophecy. Surely, my end times interpretive framework was incorrect. It was very much a form of circular reasoning:

> *The Jewish people are God's chosen people.*
>
> *The Bible says Israel is God's chosen people and that God would restore them to land in the last days.*
>
> *The restoration of Israel in 1948 was a miracle proving that the Jewish people are God's chosen people.*
>
> *We know that these are the last days because God restored Israel to the land in 1948.*

Christian Zionists often point to the "miraculous" establishment of the state of Israel in 1948 as evidence that God is fulfilling his covenant promises to the Jewish people by restoring them to the land of Israel. The argument seems compelling. The rebirth of the state of Israel in recent history is undeniably a remarkable event.

The question, however, is whether or not the rebirth of the state of Israel proves that the prophecies regarding the restoration of the Jewish people to the land constitute a fulfillment of the promises to Abraham. The answer, I believe, is unequivocally "No." Despite the profound significance of these events for some within the Jewish community, they do not affect our understanding of Scripture. After all, if I have argued correctly, the promises to Abraham have been fulfilled in Jesus and, through the Spirit, they continue to be fulfilled in the life of the people of God today. This fulfillment will climax with the descent of the new Jerusalem.

THE MIRACLE OF THE 1948 WAR

Christian Zionists bolster their conviction that God restored the Jewish people to the land in 1948 by pointing to the miraculous outcome of Israel's military victory in the 1948 war. The argument gains strength by an appeal to the fact that many Jewish people had just three years earlier survived the Nazi Holocaust. Yet, the newly formed Jewish army somehow overcame the onslaught of

The Miracle of 1948?

Arab armies from the surrounding nations. There is no question, it is argued, that the Jewish victory in war must have been enabled by the hand of God.

The problem with this appeal is that it simply does not align with the evidence. Military historians affirm that in virtually every respect, the Israeli military was superior to that of the surrounding Arab nations.[2] The newly formed state of Israel had benefited from more than a decade of training provided by British forces. They had received arms from the West and Russia. As historian Jerome Slater concludes, "The Israeli army won because it had more troops, better training, and more weapons."[3]

---

2. It was later revealed that Israel had brokered a deal with Jordan. Jordan would stay out of the war, and they would receive control of the West Bank in return. Had Jordan entered the war, the balance of power would not have leaned towards Israel—at least not as dramatically as it did.

3. Slater, *Mythologies Without End*, 76.

12

DID GOD RESTORE ISRAEL TO THE LAND IN 1948?

I HAVE ARGUED THAT the fulfillment of God's promises of family and land to Abraham and his descendants cannot be divorced from the missional call for Israel to be a light to the nations. In my opinion, the failure to acknowledge this missional role for Israel is a critical flaw within Christian Zionism. God's covenant promises cannot be separated from the missional call of making God known to the nations. This is evident from the fact that in the Old Testament, the people of Israel and later Judah were expelled from the land for disobedience to the covenant. This raises another critical objection to the Christian Zionist contention that God brought the Jewish people back to the land in 1948. Namely, if God expelled the Old Testament people of God ("Israel")[1] from the land for covenant disobedience, then does not the restoration of the people of God require covenant obedience? Since it is apparent that the

1. Even here, the problematic nature of the term "Israel" is evident. The designation "Israel" has numerous meanings in Scripture. 1) It may refer to Jacob whose name was changed to "Israel" (Gen 32:24–32); 2) It becomes the name for the children of Israel; 3) Later, it becomes name for the northern tribes as distinct from the southern tribes of Judah; 4) It can be used as a geographic location—i.e., "the land of Israel"; 5) It appears to distinguish the faithful from the unfaithful—as in Paul's designation, "they are not all Israel who are *descended* from Israel" (Rom 9:6).

modern nation-state of Israel does not represent the repentant people of God, the restoration has not taken place.

Some Christian Zionists respond by arguing that the Scriptures predict the restoration of the Jewish people first, followed by a subsequent restoration to the covenant. I find this reasoning incredulous. The expulsion of the people from the land for disobedience underscores that occupying the land is contingent upon obedience.

DOES THE RESTORATION PRECEDE REPENTANCE?

A common argument in some Christian Zionist circles is that when the Old Testament prophets indicate that God will restore the Jewish people to the land, he will do so without them having repented first. Christian Zionists appeal to passages such as Ezek 36:24–28[2] to argue that the prophet indicates that God will restore the people to the land and "then" he will sprinkle clean water on them.

The argument is that they will repent after they return to the land but not necessarily before. I note several things in response.

For one, this argument contradicts the nature of the covenant. The possession of the land is contingent on obedience. This is made explicit when God expelled Israel (the northern tribes) and later Judah (the southern tribes) from the land. Daniel's prayer in Daniel 9 recognizes that repentance precedes restoration. The argument that Ezekiel intends for us to understand that restoration precedes repentance cuts across the grain of the covenant. To suppose that the restoration in Ezekiel 36 is otherwise would necessitate a lot more than the simple order of words within the prophet's oracle. After all, one may reasonably assume that Ezekiel, like Daniel, believed repentance was necessary. There is simply no justification for supposing otherwise.

---

2. I cited Ezekiel 36:24–28 at the opening of this chapter.

In addition, the notion that Ezekiel 36 suggests that the restoration precedes repentance is tenuous at best. After all, Ezekiel suggests that God will take them from the nations to their land (Ezek 36:24) and "sprinkle clean water on you, and you will be clean" (Ezek 36:25). To suppose that this happened independently of repentance, or that the repentance happened sometime later, is pure speculation. The natural reading of the text may well indicate that this is all part of the restoration.

Furthermore, the New Testament affirms that repentance is necessary for covenant blessing. As I noted above, Jesus' first words in the Gospel of Mark are an appeal for the people to repent that they may enter the kingdom of God: "Now after John had been taken into custody, Jesus came into Galilee, preaching the gospel of God, and saying, 'The time is fulfilled, and the kingdom of God is at hand; repent and believe in the gospel'" (Mark 1:14–15). The fact that the New Testament emphatically affirms that repentance is necessary to enter the kingdom of God mitigates the notion that the restoration of God's people will precede repentance. If the prophets expected otherwise, we should rightly suppose that the New Testament would affirm this. Instead, the New Testament affirms that entrance into the kingdom depends on repentance.

Finally, I would argue that the restoration of Israel is what the New Testament is about. This is evident in that the first words of Jesus in the Gospel of Mark are, "The time is fulfilled, and the kingdom of God is at hand; repent and believe in the gospel" (Mark 1:15). Jesus is announcing that the kingdom of God has come and that entrance into the kingdom is predicated on repentance.[3] If this is so, then the New Testament appears to be announcing that the kingdom of God has come and that repentance is how one enters. And if that is so, the restoration began with the coming of Christ. There are ample reasons to suggest that the story of the Gospels is the story of God restoring his people in fulfillment of Ezekiel's prophecy. The Gospel of Mark opens with a citation from Isaiah

---

3. The key is that the offer of repentance is available to everyone. That is, it includes the nations.

40:1–3,[4] and the promise of restoration as in Ezekiel 36. Jesus, in accord with the covenant stipulations, commands everyone to repent (Mark 1:14–15).[5] That the coming of the Holy Spirit in Acts 2 fulfills the promise of Ezekiel 36:27, "I will put My Spirit within you" is virtually unquestionable. Jesus certainly fulfills other elements of Ezekiel's prophecy. For instance, he then suffers and rises from the dead: the dry bones have come to life as in Ezekiel 37. Jesus is certainly the "servant David" who "will be king over them" (Ezek 37:24). There is little doubt that the Gospel of John writes with the understanding that Jesus and the Spirit whom he sent is the fulfillment of the restored temple in Ezekiel 40–48. This is especially evident in the abundant water imagery in the Gospel of John and the parallels with Ezekiel 47:1–12.

Consequently, there is no reason to suppose that the promise of restoration of the people of God occurs independently of repentance.

---

4. Technically Mark 1:2–3 is a composite citation from Isaiah, Malachi, and Exodus.

5. John the Baptist's ministry of baptizing with a baptism of repentance (Luke 3:3) occurs at the beginning of all four Gospels.

13

CONCLUSION

FOR THE PAST SEVERAL years, I have been in conversations with some of the leading Christian Zionists and non-Zionist Christian scholars in the US and abroad. In the days following October 7, the conversations intensified—primarily through lengthy email exchanges. From the very beginning, many of us raised serious concerns about Israel's impending assault on Gaza.

Nonetheless, some of our dialogue partners were quick to defend the legitimacy of Israel's assault on Gaza. It was asserted that "Israel has a right to defend herself." Others claimed that "Israel's response is acceptable in light of the just war theory." Still others suggested that "Israel cannot make peace with the Palestinians because it does not have a legitimate partner to negotiate with." As a result, some resigned themselves to conclude, "Israel has no choice but to eliminate Hamas." On more than one occasion, I reiterated what many others were expressing, "It is not possible to eliminate Hamas. Hamas is an ideology."[1]

There is no question that Hamas is a terrorist organization whose stated goal is the destruction of the state of Israel. My concern, however, is that these arguments come across more like a concession to the world's ways and as a betrayal of the kingdom

---

1. See my livestream with Palestinian legal authority Jonathan Kuttab on the Determinetruth YouTube page: search the playlist "Israel-Gaza War."

of God. Instead of Christian leaders advocating for a just peace and a nonviolent solution—which was ultimately in the best interest of Israel also—the sentiment became, "Israel has no choice but to go after Hamas." This conviction continued to be iterated even when many of us expressed concerns that the death toll would be catastrophic.

As I write, we are over seven months into this war, and Israel has, according to their own estimates, only managed to eliminate approximately one-third of Hamas's operatives in Gaza. Not only have they failed to destroy Hamas, but we must ask if their assault on Gaza has served to strengthen Hamas. After all, how many of the seventeen thousand newly made orphans will Hamas succeed in radicalizing over the next number of years? Hamas is an ideology predicated on resistance to oppression. As long as the state of Israel uses violence against the people of Gaza, this oppression will only serve to further the aims of Hamas.

Furthermore, some of Hamas's leaders are not even in Gaza. I was stunned when I mentioned this to an influential Christian Zionist leader, and it made no difference in his thinking. "Hamas must be destroyed," he affirmed. "But it can't be destroyed," I reiterated, "It is an ideology. And besides that, some of its key leaders are not even in Gaza." He responded, "Well, Israel still has to try." I wanted to cry.

Has the church wholly capitulated to the ways of the world? Have we disregarded our missional responsibility to advocate for a just peace for the sake of everyone?

In closing, I want to reiterate that the ethics of the kingdom of God transcend one's view of Israel and the Bible. We cannot abandon the ethics of the kingdom or adopt a secondary ethic that applies only to God's chosen people. The command to love our neighbors and our enemies does not take a back seat to our love for the people of God—regardless of whether or not we believe that the Jewish people remain God's chosen people.

RESOURCES

THERE ARE AN ABUNDANCE of excellent resources available. To begin with:

Determinetruth.com has a host of resources: Use the QR code to access the website

The Determinetruth YouTube channel: Use the QR code to access the channel. Don't forget to "subscribe" to be alerted to future events.

- We produced a five-part livestream series (thirty to forty-five minutes each) to serve as an introduction to the Israel-Palestine conflict. The first three livestreams discuss the historical context from roughly 1900 to the present. Episodes four (A & B) and five look at the justice issues surrounding the conflict.

Resources

- Go to the Determinetruth YouTube page and search for the playlist "Introduction to Israel-Palestine Conflict," or go to https://www.youtube.com/playlist?list=PLn2HzYjjSLcw7Y5qDvn9Y1XJRPDnn56sZ.

- We also have fifteen to twenty livestreams discussing the present conflict in Gaza. These episodes include interviews with leading voices such as Greg Khalil, Jonathan Kuttab, Mae Cannon, Bruce Fisk, Gary Burge, David Crump, Darrell Bock, and a host of others. Go to the Determinetruth YouTube page and search for the playlist "Israel-Gaza War," or go to https://www.youtube.com/playlist?list=PLn2HzYjjSLczxH5g-r23P0DUtBlKXEEQo.

The Determinetruth blog (hosted by Patheos): use the QR code to access the blog:

- We have a long list of posts on the Israeli-Palestinian conflict going back to 2015. Go to Determinetruth.com and click on the blog tab. Then scroll down on the page and click on the Israel-Palestine picture under the blog archives.

Christian Forum on Israel-Palestine: This brand new forum has a host of excellent resources coming live in 2024, including interviews with Ilan Pappe, Ali Abunimah, and many more.

RECOMMENDED READING: IN ORDER OF RECOMMENDATION AND BY TOPIC

Aiken, Mercy, and Bishara Awad. *Yet in the Dark Streets Shining: A Palestinian Story of Hope and Resilience in Bethlehem.* Durango, CO: CliffRose, 2021. Fantastic work telling the story of Bishara Awad, the founder of Bethlehem Bible College.

Resources

Chacour, Elias. *Blood Brothers*. Old Tappan, NJ: Revell, 1984. Fr. Chacour tells his story of growing up in the Galilee. He begins in 1948 when he was eight years old and his village was destroyed by the Israeli forces.

Awad, Alex. *Palestinian Memories: The Story of a Palestinian Mother and Her People*. Bethlehem: Bethlehem Bible College, 2008. Recounts Awad's own story and how his mother raised seven children after his father was killed in 1948.

THEOLOGY OF THE LAND AND GEOPOLITICS

Burge, Gary. *Whose Land? Whose Promise?* Cleveland: Pilgrim, 2020. Updated ed. Excellent work. Perhaps the best read for understanding the conflict as a whole.

ESCHATOLOGY

Dalrymple, Rob. *Understanding the New Testament and the End Times: Why It Matters*. 2nd ed. Eugene, OR: Wipf and Stock, 2018. I argue that the entire New Testament must be read from an eschatological perspective.

MOVIES AND DVDS

See JustVision.org for a host of videos.

5 Broken Cameras. A documentary that records the nonviolent struggles of Bil'in. The film was shot almost entirely by Palestinian farmer Emad Burnat, who bought his first camera in 2005 to record the birth of his youngest son.

Budrus. An excellent documentary that details the nonviolent reaction of the citizens of Budrus and their efforts to alter the course of the separation barrier that threatened to cut off much of their olive groves and city.

Encounter Point. Tells the story of an Israeli settler, a Palestinian, a bereaved Israeli mother, and a Palestinian bereaved brother who risk it all to bring an end to the conflict.

Little Town of Bethlehem. A fantastic documentary that follows three young men (a Jew, a Muslim, and a Christian) and their efforts to bring peace.

Miral. The story of a Palestinian girl who grows up the midst of the Israeli-Palestinian conflict.

Resources

ADDITIONAL WEBSITES

https://neme.network/. The NEME website has a host of webinars, blogs, and other resources. Click on the "resources" tab.

https://electronicintifada.net/. The Electronic Intifada has done extensive work covering the war on Gaza.

http://www.dci-palestine.org/. An international organization fighting for the rights of Palestinian children.

ISRAELI PEACE AND HUMAN RIGHTS GROUPS

www.icahd.org/. Israeli Committee Against House Demolition, a nonviolent, direct-action group originally established to oppose and resist Israeli demolition of Palestinian houses in the occupied territory.

https://www.alhaq.org/. Working for Palestinian human rights. Jonathan Kuttab.

www.btselem.org/. B'Tselem, an Israeli organization concerned with the abuse of Palestinian human rights in the occupied territory.

CITED SOURCES

Beale, G. K. *The Temple and the Church's Mission*. Downers Grove, IL: InterVarsity, 2004.

Caynor, Kristin. "Christ Our Peace: Violence, Shame, and Glory in Early Christian Reception of Ephesians 2:11–22." Journal for the Study of the Bible and Violence 1 (2022) 65–94.

Dalrymple, Rob. *Revelation: A Love Story*. Eugene, OR: Cascade, 2024.

———. *Revelation and the Two Witnesses*. Eugene, OR: Wipf and Stock, 2011.

———. *These Brothers of Mine: A Biblical Theology of Land and Family and a Response to Christian Zionism*. Eugene, OR: Wipf and Stock, 2015

———. *Understanding the New Testament and the End Times: Why It Matters*. Eugene, OR: Wipf and Stock, 2018.

Moore, Russell. "'Bothsidesism' About Hamas Is a Moral Failure." *Christianity Today*, October 12, 2023. https://www.christianitytoday.com/2023/10/israel-hamas-russell-moore-moral-terrorist/.

Rydelnik, Michael. *Understanding the Arab-Israeli Conflict*. Chicago: Moody, 2007.

Slater, Jerome. *Mythologies Without End: The US, Israel, and the Arab-Israeli Conflict, 1917–2020*. Oxford: Oxford University Press, 2020.

Smith, Robert O. *More Desired than Our Owne Salvation: The Roots of Christian Zionism*. Foreword by Martin E. Marty. Oxford: Oxford University Press, 2013.

www.ingramcontent.com/pod-product-compliance
Lightning Source LLC
Chambersburg PA
CBHW032234080426
42735CB00008B/845